I0054099

Reviews of 'From Technocr[

If you have ever been thrust into that difficult situation of having to take on a leadership role for the very first time, and with little understanding of what that role entails, here's a book that has just come to your rescue.

In *From Technocrat to Leader*, Donald Gordon explains the difference between technical skills and people skills, and highlights how the ability to build trust, the capacity to develop an effective workplace culture and being able to empower others is central to becoming a great leader.

Whether you are teacher moving into a principalship, a salesperson about to take on the position of sales manager, or even a lawyer who is about become a managing partner, this book will boost your chances of a successful debut in your new role, and will allow you to fast track the development of a range of critical attributes and capabilities which are often neglected by leaders and managers new to their roles.

— Emeritus Professor Gary Martin, CEO of the Australian Institute of Management WA.

It is with great pleasure, in my role as the AusIMM President for 2019 and 2020, that I provide this book review for a long-term Institute Member and Fellow, Donald Macrae Gordon (Don).

In his book titled *From Technocrat to Leader — The essence of leadership and the rewards of earning trust and showing care*, Don provides practical and personal guidance to all people who are on the path to becoming leaders.

As engineers we generally learn how to solve puzzles and

the answers to complex questions. What we don't often learn is how to ask the right questions, to have emotional intelligence and how to be good leaders.

This knowledge deficit can result in difficulties later in our careers if not addressed.

Don quite rightly focuses his narrative on the foundations of leadership — trust and care – as all other aspects of successful leadership rely on the application of these fundamentals.

There is discussion of the particular challenges that technically-trained people face in becoming leaders, and how to overcome these difficulties.

Short but practical exercises are provided at the end of each chapter to reinforce the learnings from the chapter and to allow the reader to reflect on their own achievements and developmental needs in that particular aspect of leadership.

Don explains that if you are to succeed as a leader your people need to trust you; this trust frees them to accept the care that you as their leader want and need to provide. The book covers in depth how to build trust, and how to carefully rebuild it if lost. It details behaviours and attitudes that can destroy trust.

Trust alone is a hollow vessel and will not motivate people to follow you. To be fully functional it must be filled with empathy, compassion and care.

Don also highlights the importance of physical and mental health, listening actively, avoiding a culture of blame and empowerment.

As well as 'the how', Don addresses 'the why' in terms of the intrinsic motivators that come from within us; determining if we are passionate about something, find it satisfying and fulfilling and want to do our best at it; the flip-side being the extrinsic motivators which are external and include appreciation, fear, financial reward, public acclaim and avoidance of adverse outcomes.

AusIMM is committed to being the trusted voice of authority and influence in the resources sector. Our purpose is to provide a platform for robust, evidence-based discussions, which help us build a better, safer, and more sustainable industry. This is more important than ever before, because the modern mining landscape has become increasingly complex. And in such a complex environment, great leadership and trust is vital.

Therefore it is timely for Don to have written and published this book at this time and I encourage current as well as emerging leaders to have a read.

— Janine Herzig. President 2019-2020, the Australasian Institute of Mining & Metallurgy.

Although framed in the context of a technologist assuming a leadership role, this book is highly relevant for all current and aspiring leaders. It hits the mark that so few books on leadership do, and there is something for everyone; from the very readable style to the end of chapter self-reflection exercises. Throughout, the text is replete with personal and historical examples that resonate and bring the issues to life. Not only does Donald Gordon tackle the thorny issue of the difference between management and leadership with aplomb, his emphasis on care and trust as pivotal aspects of true leadership is both incisive and refreshing. This book is a must have for anyone in a leadership role now, or who aspires to be a good leader in the future.

— Michael Pert, AM, author and retired military intelligence officer.

In my studies I read many books on management but none quite like this one. The author, Donald Macrae Gordon provides candid examples of actions he had taken as a manager. Some are great successes others are disasters. For each he provides the behavioural principal involved and a checklist of questions for the reader to apply to their organisation. As I progressed chapter by chapter I could readily identify similar instances I had encountered.

As an Organisational Psychologist I worked with leading world authorities in change management and managed change programs in many of Australia's leading organisations. Basically my approach was to find out what is wrong, help those involved to fix it and recognise and reward their efforts. It is a self-managed program as is Donald's and the behavioural principles are the same.

I believe the book provides readers with a great and easy to apply learning experience.

— Frank L. Spencer, BCom. MA-Organisational Psychology, Fellow Aust. Inst. of Managers and Leaders, Fellow Aust. Inst. of Management Consultants.

This mostly ignored but vital subject is given an expert treatment by a writer who clearly demonstrates that he knows and understands the frustrations caused when a technical person tries to handle staff without the awareness and training to be a manager.

As a self-help book, *From Technocrat to Leader* fills the educating role extremely well with many anecdotes to illustrate the pitfalls awaiting a new technical person placed in charge of staff.

The Author also highlights the appalling lack of people handling skills in the curricula of most technical training courses.

Should be on the 'must-read' list of every manager, regardless of background or training.

Well-written and easy to follow.
— Ian Dolby, author of the 'Firebird' series.

What an incredible insight Donald Gordon offers readers throughout his book *From Technocrat to Leader*. This book clearly addresses key core values all workplaces should adopt to provide a trustworthy, safe and caring environment. I would even go so far to say that educating our future corporate leaders, middle management and supervisors may begin by using the guidelines listed within this book. A valuable source of information, experience and reference material all companies would find beneficial to have at their fingertips.
— Maureen Carolan, author of *A Clear Vision: Seeing the Invisible*.

When the transcript arrived, & having been a leader/manager/practitioner in the education & care field for many years, I really wasn't enthusiastic about reading yet another 'how to' training manual. However, I was pleasantly surprised at how easy this work is to read. I found it to be free of jargon, well structured, full of extremely salient points with plenty of relevant examples. The author's use of personal experiences is well balanced with equal amounts of failures as well as successes. I particularly appreciated his reference to emotional intelligence, trust, safety, care & humility, all of which I believe, are the basic building blocks for life skills & relationships, and not just leadership & management. Donald Macrae Gordon's manual is an excellent guide for aspiring leaders & an equally good 'go to' reference book for those who have been leaders for some time.
— Kate Clements, author of *A Flight Against All Odds – Scotland to Australia in 1968*.

An insightful, honest account of the integrity, compassion and work ethics required in Leadership roles. A must read, filled with invaluable, hands on experiences and inspirational advice for success in any field.

— Vivian Waring, author of *When Tears Ran Dry*.

Never in a million years, when I set off to read the book, *From Technocrat to Leader*, did I envisage I would find a 2 000 year old adage from the Bible as the crux of this text. – the golden rule of life -" Do unto others as you would have them do unto you."

Eminent academic, Donald Macrae Gordon, has given every aspiring leader a text book that is beautifully set out, easy to read and simply progresses his thoughts on how to move to being a good leader. He builds on trust and the culture of an organisation, and at the end of each chapter, gives us some tasks to accomplish on the road to becoming a good leader.

This book should be essential reading for everyone in business, corporations, and yes, even politicians. The propositions put forth follow a logical procession, and discuss many topics including, ethics, appreciation of the workforce, consultation, worker's physical and mental health and many more. It is enhanced by the author's personal experiences and personal growth.

As a final affirmation of this book, I leave you with the two thoughts –"Don't be a bull in a china shop," and "always do what you say you will do!"

— Judith Flitcroft, author of *Walk Back in Time*.

FROM
TECHNOCRAT
TO
LEADER

The essence of leadership and the rewards
of earning trust and showing care

DONALD MACRAE GORDON
M. Eng., FAIM, FAusIMM

ABOUT THE AUTHOR

Donald Macrae Gordon is a consultant, author, lecturer and mentor based in Perth, Western Australia. He has held numerous leadership and senior management roles, has been a thought leader in several industries and has lived and worked in five countries. He is a Fellow of the Australian Institute of Management WA and a Fellow of the Australasian Institute of Mining and Metallurgy. In 1993 he was awarded a Master of Engineering degree by the University of Melbourne for significant innovations in the mining industry.

Published in Australia by Sid Harta Publishers Pty Ltd,
ABN: 34 632 585 203
17 Coleman Parade, GLEN WAVERLEY VIC 3150 Australia
Telephone: +61 3 9560 9920, Facsimile: +61 3 9545 1742
E-mail: author@sidharta.com.au

First published in Australia 2019
This edition published 2019
Copyright © Donald Macrae Gordon 2019
Cover design, typesetting: WorkingType (www.workingtype.com.au)

The right of Donald Macrae Gordon to be identified as the Author of the Work has been asserted in accordance with the Copyright, Designs and Patents Act 1988.

The Author of this book accepts all responsibility for the contents and absolves any other person or persons involved in its production from any responsibility or liability where the contents are concerned.

All rights reserved. No part of this publication may be reproduced, stored in a retrieval system, or transmitted, in any form or by any means without the prior written permission of the publisher, nor be otherwise circulated in any form of binding or cover other than that in which it is published and without a similar condition being imposed on the subsequent purchaser.

Gordon, Donald Macrae
From Technocrat to Leader
ISBN: 978-1-925230-71-0
pp262

ACKNOWLEDGEMENTS

I thank the founder of Sid Harta, Kerry Collison, for creating an innovative business model that fosters the publication of worthwhile works that might not otherwise see the light of day.

I thank all the people who reviewed the various iterations of my manuscript, gave me encouragement and provided valuable insights that I was too close to the subject to see: my editor Kristen Rohde, book designer Luke Harris, Professor Steven Malone, University of Wolverhampton, UK, Professor Rune By, University of Stavanger, Norway, my wife Lorraine, my children Samantha, Amanda and Richard, my son-in-law Brad Lenton and Lt. Cmdr. USN (Ret'd.) Charles Gates McElwee.

CONTENTS

Introduction

I have written this book for technically trained people who aim to become leaders.

I made this transition myself; I started my career as a technical person with few people skills and a very limited understanding of what a leader is and does. Over time I came to understand and apply the truths of leadership and I became a leader.

As a freshly minted engineer I wasn't even a good manager. I was heavily focused on technical matters. I can now see that I was a technocrat — someone who believes in the supremacy of technical experts — and that I didn't appreciate the importance of people. I believed that with my first-rate technical education I had everything I needed to succeed in my career and my life. The reality proved to be very different.

If you have people working for you, you are a leader whether you think so or not. Only when you acknowledge this can you begin to think and act like a leader.

To become a leader, I had to change fundamentally. I observed and analysed the process as I went through it; I was privileged to have a number of moments of enlightenment that gave me an understanding of two universal truths of leadership that form the basis of this book.

The first is that if you are to be an effective leader, your people need to trust you. The book contains an extensive discussion of trust — what it is, how to build and maintain it and what to do if it has been lost.

The second is that once your people trust you, you can show them care and equally importantly they can accept and appreciate that care. This brings about a sense of enfoldment in them and generates enormous loyalty and all the things that go with it. There are lots of stories in the book about this.

You need to understand what a leader is and how leaders differ from managers. I cover this in detail. Many people progress to become managers but in my experience far fewer become first-rate leaders.

When I reflected on the path I took to becoming a leader, I realised that in some ways my strong technical education was an impediment. It subtly conditioned me to intellectualise the learning process and to believe that the only worthwhile learnings were those that came via my brain. I concluded that this was not the case (see Chapter 4).

I believe that as leaders our hearts play as big a role as our heads. As a leader we need to use our heart to empathise with what others are feeling so we can respond accordingly.

It may be that in our world, dominated by technology, many people consider that there is no longer room for the heart. My experience and belief is that this is not the case; if anything, our hearts have a bigger role to play than ever.

I deal extensively with the importance of culture and how leaders inevitably shape and set the culture of an organisation, a department or even just the section for which they are responsible. This is a default aspect of leadership; as a leader you set the culture for those you lead, whether you do it intentionally or not.

My experience of successfully motivating many people is that an individual will do his or her best if you as their leader remove what hinders and frustrates them (see Chapter 15).

Whilst I have written the book primarily in the context

of work, what you learn from it may also help you in your private life. A psychologist was providing me with feedback on a psychometric test I had taken. As we talked, I told her about this book that I was writing. I explained that I started my career as an engineer and a technocrat, but my education didn't give me people skills. She said: 'I know exactly what you mean; I'm married to one of those!'

This book is a practical guide to what you need to do to turn yourself into a leader. It is based on my experience of what works.

The book deals with the personal aspects of leadership, not the development of vision or strategy that leaders must undertake.

I have included many stories from my past. Some deal with difficult experiences I had on the road to becoming a leader. There are also many stories of how my working life changed dramatically for the better once I started doing what I needed to do. During the periods I describe, although I was grappling with becoming a leader, my professional work was going extremely well. My clients were very happy, and these were fertile periods during which I came up with a number of innovations that remain at the global cutting edge to this day.

Come and join me on my journey to leadership.

Chapter 1

Technical skills vs. people skills

I was an only child. Perhaps that's where the trouble started! I think that in childhood I didn't acquire the social skills that children with siblings do.

At the age of eighteen and straight out of high school I started university. Four years later I emerged with an honours degree in engineering tucked under my arm and I set off on my career believing I knew everything I needed to know.

I was very confident. Engineers need to be confident. We design, build and maintain the complex structures on which people's lives depend so our technical education is very thorough and we graduate with strong self-belief.

However, in four years of tertiary study I received very little training in managing or leading people. In the one session on the subject that I recall, we were invited to analyse a number of practical people-management scenarios that I could see might crop up in my work. In a one-hour session it was not possible to do more than skate across the subject. I had a distinct feeling of unease at the thought of being so ill-prepared for certain aspects of what lay ahead. The feeling passed and I forgot about it, only to have it forcibly brought back when I started work and began to encounter people management challenges.

The small content of people management compared to the technical content in my course coloured my perception at a subconscious level about the relative importance of people and leadership skills compared to technical skills. It helped shape a view that my technical skills alone would be enough. Supporting this conclusion was my faith in the prestigious university I attended, to help me acquire the right balance of skills to take forward.

It may be that in structuring my course, the university assumed that I would acquire management and leadership training after I started working and as such the absence of training in leadership wasn't an omission. But it certainly influenced my perception.

In the next chapter I discuss what a leader is and what the differences are between leaders and managers.

Exercises

→ Did your education give you a good grounding in how to lead people or was it too heavily focused on your acquisition of technical skills?

→ Do you know a manager who has strong technical skills but is lacking in leadership skills?

→ How does this imbalance affect the manager's performance?

Chapter 2

Leaders and managers

I spent time lecturing in the business school of a UK university. I asked a group of my leadership students who were already in employment to rate their managers on a scale from one to ten. The responses mostly sat between five and seven but ranged from plus ten to minus ten! I then asked the people whose responses were at the extremes of the range to explain how they came up with their ratings. I was particularly interested in the reasons for the strong negative ratings; they were consistently 'cannot be trusted', 'doesn't care about us', 'manages reactively', 'has their favourites who always get the plum jobs', and so on. You can imagine how much resentment these managers generated and the effect it had on their relationships and ability to do their jobs. The highly rated managers — the leaders — exhibited very different traits.

"Manager" is a common enough job title. You will rarely find the word leader in a job title. "Leader" might be used as a functional title, for example "team leader" but in this case the reference is to running and organising a team. More often than not such people are just supervisors, doling out and overseeing tasks and not necessarily having to manifest the traits of a leader.

To be an effective manager you need an extensive skill

set. That is not the theme of this book so I won't focus on it, however as a guide you will need:

- ▶ A first-rate grasp of the fundamentals and technical aspects of your department.

- ▶ An understanding of the company's expectations in regard to the required nature and timing of your department's outputs.

- ▶ An understanding of how your department fits in with other departments.

- ▶ An ability to plan activities and anticipate and prepare for upcoming requirements.

- ▶ An ability to focus on detail as well as on the larger realities.

- ▶ An ability to shift your focus rapidly to areas that require attention.

- ▶ An ability to 'keep all the balls in the air' so that nothing is neglected.

- ▶ A commitment to close tasks out in a timely manner.

- ▶ Intuition about anything that is not right so you can intervene and fix it before it goes off the rails.

If you're a manager of people, you're a leader, and while

management and leadership have elements in common, they're not the same. You need to be aware of the differences. I believe that a lack of understanding of the differences between managers and leaders hinders managers from making the leap to becoming leaders.

With your technical training you probably started your career in a purely technical role with no direct reports (people reporting directly to you). In time you were promoted to supervisor then eventually to manager, gaining direct reports as you went. At each step the leadership and management of people became a bigger part of your job and the technical aspects increasingly became the province of your reports. So you approached management from a technical perspective not a leadership perspective. In fact your ongoing technical involvement and immersion in day-to-day operational matters probably kept you pointed in the technical direction and away from leadership. That was certainly true of me.

As a manager with a team working for you, you're responsible for the functioning of your department or section but for the most part your people perform the functions. So you're actually a manager of people, hence you're a leader. This is so whether you believe it or like it or not. You can pretend that the leadership aspect doesn't exist, ignore it and just be a manager. But to be an effective leader you need to do things differently and to do different things to what a manager does. If you do not embrace the leadership aspect you will not do well at leading people. Even if you're a first-rate manager in other respects, your life will be a struggle on the people side if you do not acknowledge and act on the needs of your leadership role. This is because you'll be like the proverbial bull in the china shop, unaware of the resentments you are creating and how these are hindering your progress.

The failure of a manager to be a leader can bring down that manager, or at best severely handicap them in what they can achieve. So why not strive to understand what being a leader means and get good at it?

Some differences between leaders and managers

Here are some important differences between leaders and managers.

A leader:	A manager:
Actively builds trust.	Is process oriented.
Is a caring role model.	Performs a role.
Determines the culture.	Works within the culture.
Inspires and motivates.	Solves problems.
Coaches and mentors.	Trains.
Has their gaze fixed over the horizon.	Has their eyes fixed on the day-to-day.
Focuses on the big picture.	Focuses on more immediate responsibilities.
Provides strategy and direction.	Follows policy and procedure.
Works to strengthen the company.	Is a functionary.

I cover in detail many of the traits and activities of leaders that are listed above, with a focus on the first five.

As a manager developing into a leader you still need to meet your management obligations. You cannot ignore the management side and just concentrate on the leadership aspects as that would be a shortcut to the exit.

Exercises

→ How do you rate yourself as a leader?

→ How do you rate yourself as a manager?

Chapter 3

Culture

What does culture mean and what is the culture of an organisation? Whole forests or their electronic equivalents have been cut down to explain culture. I will use a simple way to illustrate it.

Culture is the atmosphere that pervades an
organisation and is the experience of working there.

It is generally accepted that the culture of an organisation is set at the very top; however, as the leader of a department, section or team you determine the culture of that department, section or team.

If you have just joined an organisation you will be keen to understand its culture; hopefully you will have tried to research it before you joined, including asking about it in your interviews. After all, you will be immersed in it so if you place high value on working in organisations with great cultures, as you should, it's important to know about it.

We can learn a lot about the culture of an organisation just by spending time in the reception area, perhaps while we wait to be interviewed. Is there a feeling of tension? How do the male members of staff speak to the female receptionist?

If bullying is a part of the culture it is often expressed toward junior female employees; we may well see it in the reception-ist's facial expression and body language when people are addressing her. Bullying is all too common. If you don't detect bullying, that is very much a tick in the box for the culture.

Are the senior leaders and managers trustworthy? This may take you a while to work out once you're on the inside. Untrustworthy people do not declare this side of themselves but over time you will be able to judge it from their behaviour.

What is the attitude of the senior leadership to safety? We hear talk of the safety culture of an organisation, however safety culture is a sub-set of the overall culture. If the overall culture is poor then it is unlikely that safety culture will be any better, because to be so it would need to be inconsistent with the rest of the organisation.

We can gain a picture of the safety culture by studying outcomes for both lead and lag indicators; if these are poor, it is likely that safety is not being given the prominence it deserves. I always ask for these statistics at interviews so I can discuss them with the interviewers.

Are accidents, incidents and near misses thoroughly inves-tigated to get to the root causes, or when an accident occurs is there a tendency to blame the individuals involved? If so, this is a black mark for the culture. The causes of accidents are complex but most often the root causes lie in the organisation itself. I cover this in detail in the section headed 'Lead and manage safety well' in Chapter 13.

If your people don't see you as having a first-rate approach to safety, they will find it difficult to trust you and they will come to believe that you don't care about them or their welfare.

The book "Failure to Learn" by Andrew Hopkins (2009) contains an excellent example of the influence of top management on safety culture even in a very large multinational corporation. This book details the investigation into the explosion at BP's Texas City Refinery in March 2005 that killed fifteen workers and injured 170. The board of enquiry took evidence from a top BP executive to the effect that the then CEO of BP, Lord John Browne, showed 'little interest in safety'. This disinterest trickled down through the hierarchy and led to bad news about safety not making its way back up the chain. In particular, the consequences of underinvestment in safety at the Texas City refinery, which were well known and understood on the site, were not communicated to the company hierarchy. This underinvestment, specifically a failure to upgrade the distillation column vent to a flare tower, was a major cause of the accident.

Culture may not be uniform throughout an organisation. In companies that have branches in widespread locations, the culture may be great in head office but may deteriorate the further out you go. It is a great achievement of leadership to maintain a consistent culture throughout far-flung operations.

Culture and leadership

As a leader you determine the culture of that part of the company for which you are responsible. If you are the company's prime leader, the chief executive, you set the culture for the whole company. If you lead a small section, you set the culture for that section; even if this is the case you can still influence the culture of your organisation more broadly.

Leaders model behaviour for those around them. For example, if leaders walk past hazards without taking action, others who see this will believe it is OK to do likewise. If top management acts in an uncaring way, others will feel this is acceptable. If leaders bully, managers and supervisors will believe it is OK to bully. A cancer will spread through the company. You can prevent this as a leader by exhibiting and condoning only behaviours you want manifested.

You may think: 'That's all very well if I'm the chief executive or a senior manager. In those roles I could certainly influence what goes on. What if I'm just a supervisor with a handful of people working for me?' Well, you're still a leader. By adopting the advice in this book, you can make a big difference to your team. You can create a culture in microcosm. You can build a team that is highly motivated, empowered, interdependent, energised by their work and their success and keen to attract other good people into the company because it's such a great place to work.

Your team can become a benchmark for how teams should be. Their example and yours can find its way into the fabric of the company, influencing for the better all who work there.

Great culture is catching. Others will ask to join your team. Managers will ask what your secret is. Your team will become known and recognised for its culture. Elsewhere I talk about other related effects; these may include the other side of the coin such as ostracism and isolation of supervisors and managers who are seen not to be treading this enlightened path.

In all these ways can a company's culture be transformed for the better.

Exercises

→ Describe the culture of that part of the company for which you are responsible. Is it open and transparent? Are people happy? Do they get on well and cooperate? Are people bullied? Do people feel threatened or fearful?

→ What behaviours do you model?

→ Have you contributed to bettering the culture? If so, how?

Chapter 4

How formal education affects the way we learn

I believe that in most cases people who are drawn to pursue a specialised education and subsequent career are likely to have certain attributes that fit them for that type of education and career. The attributes make it likely that these people will develop into competent and effective managers.

However, in my experience people who become managers after training in a specialisation can be at some disadvantage when it comes to developing into leaders.

When I reflected on the path I took to becoming a leader, I realised that a technical education is a less-than-ideal preparation for leadership. The difficulty is that technical training can subtly condition us to believe that for something to be of value it must come to us via our intellect; we learn to intellectualise everything, to value intellect above all else and to shy away from learning opportunities that come from other sources. What a pity.

If you've undergone a rigorous and lengthy education, you have necessarily internalised a way of acquiring new skills that reflects the way you were learning during your training. If, as I did, you spend four or more years learning in a certain way, that way is likely to become your default way. This is further reinforced every time you take another training course.

Formally trained managers can view leadership as just another bolt-on skill like learning to use a new piece of software. While certain aspects of leadership can be learned, the indispensable element of leadership is empathy — the ability to put oneself in another person's shoes and feel what they are feeling. This is a heart function not a head function and requires a fundamentally different approach. If you aspire to lead people and not just to manage them, you need empathy. Fortunately, as humans, we come with empathy built in. But it's like a muscle; it becomes atrophied from lack of use and you must exercise it to strengthen it.

A habituated formal style of learning can narrow people's focus and blind them to lessons they can draw from their experiences. Those people may discount or ignore such opportunities. Yet some of my most profound learnings have come from experiences. One such event was the "ah-ha moment" I had in Chile that I talk about in Chapter 14. That was a moment where I took a step back from something that had happened in my work and saw it for the profound lesson it held for me.

In these times of increasing specialisation, many companies have lots of technical specialists. Companies in some industries are primarily composed of technical specialists, all immersed in the demanding technical aspects of their roles. In these environments each person models the highly technical approach of those around them and an empathetic leader may feel out of place; in fact, such a person may not ever get hired. However, that does not reduce the need for a leader to have empathy. It could be said that in such environments a leader's empathy is all the more important, as it may be a rare commodity.

The technical realm contains more absolutes than the

people realm. Either that steel beam is strong enough or it's not. There's a certainty to the answer provided the correct procedure has been used to design and construct the beam and it is used within its limitations. Technical training, followed by using the skills acquired in everyday work, gives people comfort in these certainties.

Moreover, technical work deals in facts not feelings. Those facts might be subject to interpretation but they're still facts. Feelings are different. Not everyone is comfortable dealing with their own or others' feelings. Yet it is an ability that can be cultivated. It's very rewarding and it's essential for people who aim to be leaders.

We default to doing what we feel comfortable doing, and we shy away from doing what we feel uncomfortable doing. For those who lack confidence in their people skills it can be easier to stick to the technical stuff, ignore the people issues and deal reactively with them when they can no longer be ignored. The author and English public servant C. Northcote Parkinson identified this phenomenon in his book *Parkinson's Law*, published in 1957. The book is written in a humorous style and you might think it is purely satirical, however Parkinson enunciated several universal truths; his book should be required reading for every leader.

Parkinson's so-called laws are statements of principle derived from his observations of human nature. You will not see results of academic research in his book, however once you're familiar with Parkinson's laws you'll see examples of them everywhere.

The best known of Parkinson's laws is that 'work expands to fill the time available'. A busy person does a task quickly because they have no choice. A person with little to occupy them takes all day to do the same task, because they can.

Another of Parkinson's laws may be paraphrased as "we default to doing what we can do and are comfortable doing, not to what we should do". Does that sound familiar?

Parkinson gives the example of a board of directors holding its monthly meeting. There are several expenditure items on the agenda varying in importance from minor to major. Little time is spent on the big-ticket item. The meeting attendees are uncomfortable discussing it and reluctant to get into the detail, so a decision is rushed through. However, a minor item — whether or not to build a bike shed for the employees — receives lengthy attention and spirited debate because everyone has an opinion and feels justified in voicing it.

An extreme example perhaps, but it illustrates Parkinson's belief that when faced with a choice, people can elect to do what they feel comfortable doing rather than addressing equally or more important issues that may be less comfortable for them.

I believe this applies to technically trained people who are learning how to lead. They're comfortable in the technical realm but when it comes to dealing with people, they don't have the same level of comfort and this can cause them to handle such situations reactively; rather than seek out people issues that may develop into problems and try to nip these in the bud, they sit back and wait until the people issues can no longer be ignored. By then, some damage has already been done and more work is needed to put everything right. This approach leads to general frustration, dissatisfaction and wasted energy.

I advise you to embrace the people side of your work using the principles set out in this book. Start with the following: before every interaction with one of your people, ask yourself if the way you plan to do it is the way you would want it done to you if the roles were reversed. Run this check every time and interact with your people only in ways that meet this high but reasonable standard.

My experience is that when you apply the principles in this book you get very good, predictable outcomes with people; this very predictability, which you will come to experience, takes much of the stress out of dealing with people.

Even psychologists, who should understand how people tick, don't necessarily know how to relate to people at a practical level. This is illustrated in the following story. A safety training company hired a senior psychologist on a short-term contract for a project. The psychologist had to cooperate with employees in the company including admin people to get the project done. Unfortunately, she had an air of superiority that caused others to resent her and to be uncooperative. The company's owner who hired her and who related this story to me watched her struggle each day and although she did her best, she was unable to help the psychologist escape from the corner into which she had painted herself.

Footnote: what are entrepreneurs like as managers?

Some of the entrepreneurs and visionaries with whom I've worked were also trying to function as managers. Each one started their company from scratch and had a vision of grandeur for it that eventually became reality. In its formative stages however, a company cannot always afford managers. During these times the leader also has to be a manager. This doesn't always work well because of the different traits required. For example, the manager needs a grasp of detail but the entrepreneur eschews detail because their vision is constantly leaping beyond the horizon. Entrepreneurs may struggle to function as managers; if you work for someone like this you may occasionally need to fill in the gaps for them!

Exercises

→ Have you ever had a manager who lacked people skills or lacked confidence in dealing with people?

→ How did these limitations affect the way that person managed and led?

→ Were you negatively impacted?

→ How many of the listed leadership attributes do you display?

→ Describe the culture of that part of the company for which you are responsible. Is it open and transparent? Are people happy? Do they get on well and cooperate? Are people bullied? Do people feel threatened or fearful? What behaviours do you model?

→ Keep a note of your conclusions so you can apply the measures I have set out.

Chapter 5

The wonder of trust

A major part of my transition to becoming a leader was learning the importance of trust and of being trusted.

Trust is a complex subject with a simple principle at its heart. Trust is increasingly being seen for its rightful place at the centre of relationships.

In my view, in these times where so many people and institutions formerly regarded as beyond reproach have been exposed as untrustworthy, trust between individuals has assumed even greater importance.

We can think of trust as 'firm belief and confidence in, and reliance on, the integrity, dependability, truthfulness and strength of someone'.

The trust I'm referring to here is the trust your people need to have in you as their leader. I deal later with the subject of how you develop and show trust for your people.

Being trusted is the key that opens all other doors. If trust is absent these doors will remain tightly locked. If people trust you, all is possible.

Building trust needs to be approached from a heart perspective, not a head perspective. I believe that a person begins to be trustworthy when they make a commitment to themselves, in their heart, to be trustworthy. If a person merely exhibits trustworthy behaviour but appears to have intellectualised it and not to have made that internal commitment, will I trust that person? Probably not, because I will see that the foundation is lacking. In the absence of this genuine foundation, I will believe that the trustworthy behaviours could stop at any time. Such a person is not truly trustworthy. The commitment comes first; behaviours that build trust follow naturally from the commitment. Incidentally, recall one useful definition of a team: a group of people who trust one another!

At first, I didn't understand the importance of trust. The pieces of the puzzle arrived in the wrong order but eventually I rearranged them and saw where they fitted.

The great importance of caring was revealed to me first. When you're ignorant of it you may have an excuse but once you understand it and feel it in your heart and in your bones you have no option from that moment on to act toward people, especially your own people, in a caring way. I cover this in great detail later in the book.

Once I understood caring I began to cast around in my store of experiences for clues as to what else was important, for I knew that caring alone was not enough. I could see that my caring acts in isolation had not been appreciated. In time I found the answer — trust.

My premise is that most people inherently want to trust; but with some, their ability to trust has been damaged over time due to betrayals big and small or from just one untrustworthy but significant act on the part of another person that has left an indelible mark. You can help these people.

If as a leader you demonstrate your trustworthiness without exception, most people will eventually come to trust you. This transition to trusting is more profound for people who have been badly betrayed and lost their ability to trust. You may earn their undying loyalty when you gain their trust.

Trust can be lost. Committing just one act that an untrustworthy person would commit may cause you to be branded as untrustworthy. Trust once lost is difficult but not impossible to rebuild. I discuss this.

If people don't trust you, your ability to lead will be severely compromised. If people do trust you, you will differentiate yourself in a very positive way. People from other departments will tell you they want to work for you and will ask you to consider them for opportunities in your department. I have had such approaches many times. Trust is not the only reason but it is an important reason. Leaders who are untrustworthy will become increasingly isolated and perhaps even ostracised by their own people who have seen from your example what they are missing out on.

If others trust you it will not be just because you are trustworthy. Trust alone is a hollow vessel and will not motivate people to follow you. To be fully functional it must be filled with empathy, compassion and care.

Consider this. An employee is talking with a colleague who has just been hired. The new hire asks what their manager is like. The other employee replies: 'Well, if she says she'll do something she always does it. So you can trust her in that way. But she doesn't really care; she wouldn't put herself out for us and she wouldn't defend us against others.' Is that a full measure of trust?

There are wonderful stories from my own working life about the power of trust and the benefits I derived as a leader from being trusted. In one management role I had responsibility for several departments including Human Resources and Industrial Relations. The labour agreement for the workers at a particular depot was coming up for renegotiation. The workforce at this depot was heavily unionised and the union members were quite militant. This workforce had a management hierarchy in the company: the depot manager who was their immediate manager, his manager who was a general manager, and his manager who was the executive general manager of that division and my peer. In the negotiations, these workers were to be represented by their union. A senior management person needed to represent the company. There were two obvious choices — the executive general manager or the general manager of the division, both of whom had line responsibility for the depot. The men wanted neither of them. Instead, through their depot manager they specifically asked if I could be the management representative even though I had no line management responsibility for them. The reason they gave was that they trusted me. What a priceless gift.

In the same organisation a mature-age employee based in a remote depot was diagnosed with cancer and given only weeks to live. As head of Human Resources, I started to deal with this man whom I had never met, to help him through the HR aspects of his unfolding tragedy. I had a number of conversations with him and he quickly asked that I, rather than one of his line managers, be his sole point of contact with the company because he trusted me to understand his plight and to respond to him with compassion.

Application of these principles should be a pure and selfless act. You treat people as you would have them treat you and this should stem from the genuine care and empathy you have for them. You know that you will reap significant rewards, but this should be secondary.

The essence of the principles is that they require you to walk in others' shoes and to feel what they are feeling. Applying these principles in a superficial way without embracing the feelings that go with them will not work. Others may not be able to put their finger on what is wrong, but they will know something is not right. You will never fully gain their trust.

In the following, I describe events that had a pivotal effect on my understanding of trust.

Some difficult lessons for me about trust

At university I had a scholarship with a major mining company. One of the conditions was that I worked for the company out on their sites during my summer vacations. After year one of study I spent a few weeks labouring (literally) in an underground coal mine; this was quite a culture shock for a lad who had led a sheltered life. The summer vacation at the end of year two saw me doing a variety of tasks at a large open cut iron ore mine a very long way from home. After year three I worked for ten weeks on a remote open cut manganese mine on an island in northern Australia. Then after finishing year four I was taken on full time at that mine as a graduate mining engineer and spent two years there. Life in this place could not have been more different to my former life in the city; I couldn't have a car, there were no single women and it didn't even have a phone to dial out. In truth, I was fairly unhappy for the two years I was there.

In this job I had people reporting to me: mine foremen (they were all men then), haul truck drivers and mobile plant operators. I received a small amount of training in people management in this role. Perhaps I would eventually have received more. In those days, companies didn't expect their managers to be people managers and leaders in the way we do now.

My next role was on the world's largest iron ore mine in a remote part of Australia managing a large off-road tyre maintenance workshop and providing technical consulting to the mine on the running of their off-road tyres. I am talking about tyres used on 120 short ton capacity trucks, tyres that in combination with their rim weigh several tons. These 120-tonners were among the biggest mining trucks of their day but are not considered large now when trucks of 400 short ton capacity are common. We had over seven hundred big off-road tyres under management. The work group under me consisted of service personnel on three shifts plus supervision and admin people.

The consulting came readily to me, but I was not so comfortable with the people side. I concentrated on the technical aspects and largely left it to the supervisors to manage the people and their issues. Looking back, I can see that they were also ill equipped to deal with people so the people management side was largely ignored or handled reactively when it could no longer be ignored.

Some of the blue-collar people who worked for me liked me, knew what I needed to do to foster better relations with my men, and were comfortable telling me. One — Lindsay B. — would come to me with suggestions like 'why don't you stroll out of the office more often and spend time with the boys in the workshop? They'd really appreciate it.' I saw the logic of this, but I didn't feel the importance of it. I do now. I did begin to circulate but it was not the only thing I needed to change. I realised later that in saying what he said, Lindsay was showing great care for me.

When it came to my people, I was reactive and I only dealt with people issues if they became a real problem. I started to notice resentment and passive resistance from some of my workforce. I well recall my approach to people in those days. I was in a position of authority but I saw it as somewhat hollow because at the time it wasn't backed up by much experience in doing the job. I didn't want my inexperience to be revealed. Perhaps I harboured a secret belief that due to my inexperience I wasn't worthy of the position, so I compensated by being more assertive. With most of my people it wasn't necessary to exert my authority but with some it was. So I did. Some people pushed back and there was ill will directed toward me from some quarters. This led to fractured relationships that were difficult to repair. I was in the dark as to the reasons and began not to enjoy what I was doing.

Only a small percentage of the people who worked for me understood, trusted or liked me. The views of the others, mainly blue-collar employees plus the supervisors, ranged from suspicion to outright enmity. Those in the latter camp would do whatever they could to unsettle me and thwart me. On one occasion one of the foremen made an allegation to a serviceman, unfounded and untrue, that I had insulted the latter's wife. His intent was to have the serviceman assault me and drive me off the site. It didn't work, but it gave me pause for thought. The foreman in question had his own agenda for trying to get rid of me, which I'll discuss in another chapter.

There were certainly good times and good relationships with some in my work group, but these were in the minority and I didn't understand what made some relationships good and others bad. However, my relationships with those closest to me, my family, were working well. Herein lay a clue because guess what? I cared deeply for those people. But I wasn't thinking from a perspective of care at that time.

This was in effect the first workforce I'd had with a fixed crew that worked directly for me or through a foreman who reported to me. I had never had a workforce with what I now recognise as high morale, so I didn't know any different and I just thought it was normal.

Other managers from our company who came to site to take over during my annual leave reported low morale in my workforce. I was inclined to view these comments as cheap shots taken in my absence, so I missed the chance to learn from them.

Because I was exceptionally good at most aspects of my job, I believe that my superiors, the owners of the company, were reluctant to take action about the morale issues. I also think that their people skills were quite limited, so they just didn't know what to do.

So I limped along. It's not easy to lead or manage a work group well in this situation. People tend to be passively unco-operative. There were enough people in the work group who were ill disposed toward me to influence those who were not. There was no open rebellion though I had my share of industrial problems. There was just a general lack of motivation and it was hard to get momentum going.

The saga of the pens

Here is a story from my past that I later saw as life changing. I cringe to think of the damage it did to my credibility and the ability of my people to trust me and to relate to me.

It happened during a later stint at the iron ore mine I described above when I was again managing the off-road tyre workshop and consulting on technical matters. One day as a cost-conscious manager (I didn't think in terms of leadership in those days) I was checking into the amount we had spent on various things and I noticed that we appeared to be going through a lot of pens — ballpoint pens that cost perhaps 30 cents each. If a service person needed a pen he would come to the office and the admin person would just give him one — no questions asked. Most times if a pen needed replacing it was because it had fallen out of the serviceman's pocket, not because our people were keeping the local black market supplied with pens.

However, I was annoyed at this wanton wastage of pens so I posted a notice in the lunch room saying that henceforth each person who needed a new pen would have to justify it by bringing in the old one to prove they needed a replacement. This severely annoyed my workforce. I was warned of industrial action if I persisted. This would not have gone down well with our mining company client given the trivial nature of the issue. So I backed down, making pens freely available again. I realised that my cost saving measure, though well-intentioned, had been misguided.

You may laugh; I can now! But I certainly wasn't laughing at the time. Having made the mistake of imposing the restrictive pen policy I then reversed it but that didn't undo the damage. Can you see why? My workforce felt that I had not seen it as a mistake, only that I had been forced to overturn it by the threat of repercussions. They saw me as a person who was still capable of doing such a thing and might do it again. So after the policy reversal their level of trust in me went down and their view of me was actually worse. They were hard-working men who didn't deserve what I had done so they had a sense of injustice as well. What a mess. I think my standing with that work group never quite recovered — all over a few dollars' worth of pens.

By my action I had further eroded trust with my people. At the time I didn't see it that way; I wasn't tuned in to trust as

I am now. I just saw it as me having done something and the work group having reacted. As mentioned earlier I didn't have good relations with the work group generally, so this incident didn't particularly stand out. Later I saw it as absolutely pivotal.

I have often applied the lessons I took from this incident. So what were they? The first and most obvious is that before I took the original decision, I should have put myself in the shoes of those who would be on the receiving end and tried to feel how they would feel. This would have told me in an instant. I could also have taken soundings from my foreman. Had I done either of these I would not have acted as I did. There would have been no situation from which to recover.

The second lesson is that having made the mistake and seen its effect, I should have acted immediately to fix the damage before negative attitudes became entrenched. I missed the opportunity to make amends. I discuss making amends in a later chapter. I believe that by making amends as soon as possible I could not only have recovered the situation, but I could have built a bond with the men and freed them to regain trust in me. I should have called a meeting with the entire work group and apologised unreservedly. I should have explained that my intent was to save money but that I was misguided to do it that way. Perhaps I could have put on a barbeque with a few drinks, made light of it. I could even have given everybody a nice pen as a gift!

Doing all this would have fixed it. People in the work group would have discussed it, said to one another that OK, I screwed up, but I was big enough to admit my mistake and put it right. I could have turned it to my advantage. But I didn't do any of that.

Finally, I needed to put my ego aside and show humility, to acknowledge my humanness and not to pretend that my rank made me superior to my people and immune to mistakes. I needed to show that I understood the Golden Rule: 'do unto others as you would have them do unto you'.

Without trust, little can be achieved and what can be done is a struggle.

People who don't trust you or worse actively mistrust you ascribe negative motives to you even when your actions have the best intent. They do this to protect themselves from harm and hurt. It's safer. They will treat the good deeds you do as exceptions. 'He did one good thing for me — so what? He still can't be trusted. He's just someone who occasionally does something good.'

All of this was very frustrating. To try to improve relations with my team I came up with the idea of sending each of the servicemen a card on their birthday. I mentioned this to one of my admin people. He advised me not to bother as no one would appreciate it coming from me.

The incident with the pens remained raw with me for many years. Eventually by analysing it I came to understand the importance of trust.

Employee expectations about trust

My theory is that many employees have a belief that management cannot be trusted. This stems from:

▶ a deep-seated subconscious belief that the ruling classes act primarily in their own interests rather than to the benefit of those they rule leading to:

→ a perception that people in authority in general cannot be trusted leading to:

☆ a conviction that people in management positions cannot be trusted.

Employees may have had bad experiences with managers who betrayed them or otherwise showed themselves to be untrustworthy. We all find ways to protect ourselves from hurt and if we have experienced betrayal we learn to trust less or perhaps not at all. It's less risky.

The subject of trust came up when I was living in the UK in 2014. In my spare time I volunteered at the local Royal Air Force air museum and when I had the time I would spend my Tuesdays working on the aircraft exhibits. One day I was chatting with a group of fellow volunteers. One elderly gentleman related the following story. As a young man he worked in a factory. One of the factory's machines was obsolete and due to be scrapped. As it had no residual value the man asked his manager if he could have it because it would be useful in his home workshop. The manager refused saying that the decision to scrap it had to stand. The employee accepted the ruling, however later that day as he was going home he saw one of the other factory workers dropping the machine off at the manager's house.

One can only presume that this manager had no concept of trust. Or perhaps he thought it was unlikely his treachery would be uncovered. It's easy to see what would have followed this incident. Our man would have been unlikely ever to trust that manager again. If this incident rankled so much that fifty years later he still told the story, it's certain that at the time it did the rounds of the workforce and effectively destroyed trust in the manager. That manager paid a high price for this one betrayal.

People who have become sceptical and untrusting are a challenge to lead. They can be particularly frustrating for a leader who knows the importance of trust and prides themselves on their trustworthiness but through no fault of their own is treated as untrustworthy. We'll discuss how to handle this situation.

The role of trust in business

You may have had an experience similar to the following. Your employer has submitted a tender for a major contract and you are on the bid team. You and the other team members are involved in a final pitch to the client's bid evaluation team. The meeting has started. The client team leader who is the decision maker is listening intently to what your colleagues say. Each speaks in glowing terms about your company's technical competence and ability to deliver. But the client seems to have drifted off, his eyes glazed over. He's not hearing what he wants to hear, the killer statement that will clinch the deal for you.

You have elected to speak last. You're different to the others on your team; you understand that initially the client evaluated the risks around your company's technical strength. Having satisfied himself about that he set about evaluating your capability to deliver. You passed that test too and you've reached the finals. Now the client is evaluating whether he can trust you. This is separate from capability — he has already established that. The client is looking for something more, something that will differentiate your company from the other bidders.

You understand the power of trust. You know that the

client is now deciding whether to entrust the contract, his company's future and his reputation to your company. At this moment it's all about trust. You know what the client needs to hear. You're about to speak. Before you begin you look the client in the eye and actively radiate the open, transparent, relaxed and trustworthy energy within you and let the client absorb it. Then you speak about trust and how important it is to everyone in your company. You assure the client that your company's commitments once given will be honoured no matter what.

You watch for the client's reaction. You sense the tension leave his body and note his expression visibly soften. You know this is what he wanted to hear.

I had this exact experience. I was the person who spoke last. We won the contract. It was the biggest in our small company's history and it was the making of us.

It may not always play out so clearly, but be mindful that in any situation where you want another person to decide something in your favour, be it a contract for your company or employment for yourself, trust will eventually play a big part in their decision.

Projecting your trustworthiness

Being trusted comes from consistently manifesting your trustworthiness through your actions and behaviour combined with projecting your trustworthiness. Trustworthiness should not be just internal to you. If it is, you're not fully benefiting from it. You can project trustworthiness wherever you go.

When I am with someone who doesn't know me well and may not yet have learned to trust me, I focus on the trustworthy energy within me (which includes the compassionate and caring aspects) and project that energy toward the other person. How do I do this? I visualise the energy physically radiating from the heart area of my body, flowing toward the other person and them absorbing it. This energy is calm, positive and confident. If this is a bit metaphysical for some readers, try it. You will be surprised at the results.

Radiating your trustworthy energy also has its uses outside the work context. I have travelled extensively internationally but have never once had my baggage searched other than where screening searches were being carried out on everyone's bags. I once travelled to a foreign country with two colleagues. What happened as we were clearing customs on arrival was instructive. One colleague made no secret of his annoyance at the customs process; the officers were very diligent in searching his bags. The other colleague had a distinctly guilty look about him so his bags were also thoroughly searched. Mine were not searched.

I didn't always radiate this energy. I have learned to do it and I've made it a habit even with people I don't know whom I encounter in daily life. It draws people to me, I think because they see something in me that they don't see in everyone. You can do it too.

In the next chapter we will explore ways to build and maintain trust.

If you can begin to *feel* these things rather than just *know* them, you are making progress.

Exercises

→ Reflect on how well people trust you. You need to be totally honest in your appraisal.

→ If the answer is "not much", consider what factors have caused trust to be lost. Later chapters will show you how to rebuild it.

→ Is there a lack of trust in management in your company? If so list the factors you believe have caused it.

→ Have you ever taken an action without adequate thought as to its consequences and seen it backfire as related above?

    → What were the effects?

    → How was people's trust in you affected?

    → Were you able to recover the situation? If so, what steps did you take?

    → What would you do differently in future?

Chapter 6

How to build and maintain trust

Trust can be built and maintained in many ways. Some important ones are listed below.

Create opportunities to build trust

When you are building a relationship and building the trust that goes with it, each party looks for signs about the trustworthiness of the other, so create opportunities to show that you can be trusted. These need not be on a monumental scale. For example, make a small commitment such as telling the other person you'll call them on a certain day at a certain time, then keep that commitment. They'll see it as evidence of your trustworthiness. Doing this is so ingrained in me that I'm no longer conscious of it. You can build to more significant actions, each time being careful to keep the commitment you've made.

A small way to build trust is to return borrowed items promptly. We've all had the experience of lending things to people then having to chase the person repeatedly to return the item. Or if you forget it's on loan you just never get it back and a long while afterwards you notice it's missing but by then you can't recall who borrowed it.

Each contact you have with a person is an opportunity to build trust — or to fritter it away if you fail to keep your side of a bargain.

Avoid doing things that damage trust

Trust is built partly by what we do and partly by what we avoid doing. Avoid actions and behaviours that destroy trust.

In my early career as a mining engineer I had responsibility for shift operations on the open-cut manganese mine I mentioned earlier. It was on a small island in a very remote location that could only be resupplied by ship or by air. This mine used large rubber-tyred front-end loaders to load ore into trucks to be taken to the crusher. Tyre stocks and ordering were not under good control and sometimes we ran out of new tyres. Due to our location these could not be obtained at short notice. They were too big to transport by air so they had to come by ship. If we ran out of tyres there were two options until new stock arrived. One was that we continued to run the loaders on their existing tyres, irrespective of condition. The other was that when the tyres wore out, especially the more critical front tyres, we stood the loaders down perhaps for weeks until new tyres arrived.

The second option wasn't too popular because it led to the mine having to reduce production. So more commonly we took the first option. It led to nail-biting situations where we were monitoring the loaders operating and watching the bald patch where the tread had worn away and the cords were exposed, grow by the hour. If a front tyre blew out when the loader had its bucket full and raised to maximum height it could potentially tip over, injure the driver and damage the machine.

In those far-off days we did more preaching about safety than managing it meaningfully. I recall that one of the mine foremen under me who had a genuine concern for his people was furious because we continued to run a loader with a front tyre that was ready to blow. He accused me of having a double standard and he was right. I now understand that his ability to trust me was badly damaged by this. I have no doubt that the workers in the mine felt the same.

In the safety context especially, if you want to bring people along with you, you must be scrupulous in walking your own talk and ensuring that your supervisors do the same. On one mine that I visited regularly in more recent years to support our workforce, there was a client-mandated target to submit one hazard report per person per week. Of course any significant hazards were reported and dealt with immediately. Each Friday one of our people took the week's hazard chits to the client safety office where they were counted. It emerged that after being counted, rather than being logged for action the chits were merely thrown away. Our people who delivered the chits saw this and it became common knowledge in our workforce.

I was outraged when I heard. I realised that legitimate safety hazards were not being properly processed and the client's action was nullifying the great work we were doing to keep our people safe. Worse was the damage to our reputation with our people if they saw us as complicit in this travesty. I continued to use the client system but in parallel I instituted an internal system where we logged all reported hazards, informed the client of them and monitored the closeout of remedial actions. By doing this I reinforced the trust our people had in us and showed them how much we cared about their welfare. I suspect I was not too popular with the client for exposing their inadequacies but I could not let our approach to risk management and safety be discredited with our people by allowing the client's actions to go unchallenged.

Always do what you say you'll do

A commitment is so easy to make but it can be so hard to keep. Many will judge your trustworthiness by how well you honour your commitments large and small.

We sometimes make commitments on the spur of the moment because someone is on our back and if we offer to do something — make a commitment — we can get them to go away. We achieve temporary relief but at the expense of having given an undertaking we may not be able to keep and perhaps having given no thought to keeping. Such commitments are best avoided as they are too easily broken and trust is lost in the process.

We often make commitments with every intention of keeping them but without having given enough thought to what is involved. I try to make commitments only after I've thought them through and am confident I can keep them.

Your failure to keep even simple and seemingly insignificant commitments may have unexpected repercussions. Consider the person to whom you make the commitment. Unless they have labelled you as unreliable and untrustworthy, they will expect you to keep your commitment. They will base some of their planning on what you have told them you'll do. They will make commitments to others based on the expectation that they'll get what you promised when you promised it. If you default, they must go to the others and unravel what they have committed to do. Their own reputation for trustworthiness is put at risk. If trust is important to them, they will not appreciate it. A commitment on which you default may have significant downstream effects that you cannot predict. You may come to be branded as untrustworthy. If you cannot keep a small commitment how will you keep a big one?

So consider your commitments carefully and make them only when you plan to keep them.

Be true to yourself

How many people are you? Are you more than one person? Do you behave differently with your superiors than you do with your team? Is there yet another persona that comes out when you're dealing with contractors and suppliers? If any of these is the case, you're not being true to yourself. I was talking with my foreman who had just attended a social function where our managing director was also a guest. My foreman commented that the MD 'can certainly put on airs and graces'. You can see where I'm going with this. Decide what your one true self is and be that person, all the time.

Behave ethically and with integrity

Ethics deals with what is right and wrong conduct. What is right or wrong might come from a consideration of what is morally right or wrong in an absolute sense or it might be viewed relative to acceptable rules or norms in the context of where it's being applied. However we define it, ethical behaviour means, for example:

- ▶ Not cheating others out of what is rightfully theirs, for example not claiming credit for others' ideas and not plagiarising their work.

- ▶ Not betraying others.

- ▶ Respecting co-workers.

- ▶ Respecting people's human rights.

- ▶ Not sabotaging others' work.

- ▶ Not misrepresenting yourself or the company.

- ▶ Not engaging in unlawful conduct.

- ▶ Honouring your commitments.

Consider how you would expect a trustworthy person to act and behave. One expectation you would reasonably have of a trustworthy person is that they should act and behave ethically. If you act and behave ethically, you are on a path to being trusted.

Here from Wikipedia is one way of looking at ethical behaviour:

Ethical behaviour is the set of standards that you hold for yourself in relation to honesty, responsibility and how you treat others in all facets of your life. The same standards are applicable to whatever position you hold in commerce, in your community and even behind your own doors where only you know what you do. Ethical behaviour means applying these standards even when it is inconvenient to do so.

Do you meet these standards? Every time? If so, well done. If not, you have work to do. Unfortunately, even unethical people will judge you adversely if you do not behave ethically.

Show respect for truth and openness

Those who honestly mean to be true, contradict them-selves more rarely than those who try to be consistent.
– Oliver Wendell Holmes.

I love the truth. The truth is what's left when everything else is stripped away — all the artifice, all the exaggeration, all the posturing, all the lies. One only has to wait, and the truth will be revealed. If as a leader you are dishonest or untruthful you will eventually be exposed, trust in you will evaporate and will be very difficult to re-establish.

By your truthful and transparent leadership, you set a high standard and a positive example for those around you.

Watch those secrets!

Related to truth and openness is the way you handle secrets.

When I refer to secrets, I'm not talking about company

information that must be kept confidential. I'm referring to situations, for example, where somebody has done something wrong but it's been covered up and those who need to know have not been informed.

If you believe that a fact can be kept secret, you are probably mistaken. Information leaks out in unexpected ways. I heard about the following that happened in a small isolated community. There was a medical clinic in the town. A teenage girl was employed to keep the patient records up to date. She went through the records, looked at people's confidential information and spread the interesting bits among her friends. You can imagine the tide of mistrust that swept through the community when this betrayal was revealed.

People pass their secrets to confidants and ask that the information go no further. Too often it does. People entrusted with a secret may pass it on because they're careless or because they don't believe it's as important as the informant claimed.

Your best strategy when you become aware of wrongdoing, once you have satisfied yourself as to its authenticity, is to report it. This sets a standard for your people. They know you will not be complicit in any cover-up. They also know you will not tolerate wrongdoing on their part and that if they behave wrongly you will expose them. By not reporting a wrongdoing you also risk being seen as complicit if the wrongdoing is exposed and it emerges, as it probably will, that you knew about it.

If you have secrets, you should assume that they will leak out. Better that you reveal the information to all rather than risk the loss of trust and reputation when it escapes and you're on the back foot trying to contain the damage.

My successor as site manager on a remote project came under pressure because the safety record among our crew had deteriorated under his management. One worker suffered a serious injury in an accident almost identical to one that had occurred previously on this manager's watch and whose causes had not been adequately addressed and rectified. The site manager tried to cover up the second accident. This was exposed and as a result he was dismissed.

The dangers of the grapevine

As a leader you need to be aware that information and rumours can proliferate on the grapevine, the unofficial communication channel that exists in all companies. The problem with the grapevine is that it invariably contains a mixture of rumour, speculation, misinformation (sometimes planted scurrilously) and mistaken belief, all coated with a dusting of truth. As such the grapevine is unreliable and dangerous as a source of information for your people. Information gleaned from the grapevine can have a veneer of authenticity about it because some will see it as the truth the company did not want revealed.

When I was training to be an airline pilot, I was taught that as captain, when you have an emergency in the air you're much better off to tell the passengers what's really going on. If you don't, their imagination will fill the gaps with possibilities that are much worse than the reality and this will cause them needless anxiety. So it is with the grapevine; fear feeds on rumour and half-truth. Also some people embellish what they hear before passing it on because they get pleasure from stirring the pot.

The moment you suspect that a particular subject has started to do the rounds of the grapevine you need to intervene quickly to provide the truth. Depending on the gravity of the situation this may mean calling special meetings that you personally address, to ensure everyone gets the truth directly from you. This gives people an opportunity to ask questions, as each person can have different fears that you don't anticipate, plus it gives you the chance to check people's body language and draw out unspoken fears. Doing all this builds trust because you're being transparent. It's also a caring act because you're relieving people of their fear and anxiety.

This direct approach also works well with the wider community including the media. There was an incident at an aged care facility in the state capital city where I lived; a resident with a skin condition was treated by being bathed in a solution containing kerosene. The media obtained the story and over a number of days drip-fed details of the alleged outrage to the public. The chief executive of the aged care facility, seeing the damage this was doing to his company's reputation, arranged to be interviewed by the media. In this widely publicised interview, he apologised for his staff's actions, stated what corrective actions had been taken and assured everyone that there would be no repeat. This halted the damaging media blitz in its tracks.

People will have justifiable concerns about anything that potentially threatens their wellbeing or security at work. So rather than waiting until you get wind of a rumour circulating, try to anticipate subjects that people may have fears about and address these with them before the grapevine has a chance to get cranked up.

Cultivate an attitude of gratitude

People love being appreciated. I was given a wonderful example of this when one of my coordinators, a lady in her fifties, was leaving the company. Her departure was not voluntary as the company was going through tough times and fixed term contract employees like her were not having their contracts renewed. Although she had only worked for me for a couple of months, I was very sorry to see her go as she had been a great help. A morning tea with around forty staff was put on to farewell her. The general manager spoke and then it was my turn. In front of the assembled throng I gave heartfelt thanks for the way she had guided me through my first weeks in the company and had been prepared to turn her hand to doing whatever I needed. By this time, she was getting a bit teary. It was her turn to respond. She thanked me for what I said then told everyone I was the best manager she had ever worked for and what set me apart was the appreciation I showed her even when in her eyes she had done nothing special. I was deeply moved that she chose to use her special moment, her opportunity to bask in the good wishes and appreciation of all, to pay tribute to me.

As we broke for morning tea another woman came up to me. Also in her fifties, she had assisted me with a project I was working on and had been very helpful. She began to tear up as she told me she had been in the company for twelve years and had never before received the level of appreciation that I showed her. She said that this had made her want to do everything possible for me.

In my mind all I had done for these two ladies was to show genuine and well-deserved appreciation for their efforts.

Genuine appreciation is a great motivator. Being appreciative is a habit that can be cultivated. Showing appreciation is also part of being humble. If you take on an air of superiority thinking that your elevated rank obliges others to serve you, you will not feel appreciative or show appreciation because you always expect people to do what they do. If people sense an expectation of them based on their inferior rank they will push back, openly or passive-aggressively. You will create resentment (see Chapter 10).

The humble person will say to themselves 'if they so choose, this person could put in less effort so I should show appreciation for what they do.' The person you thank for their efforts may say 'I was only doing my job' but they will smile to themselves because they appreciate the recognition.

Some managers may withhold appreciation because they believe the person to whom they show it will try less hard in future. My experience suggests otherwise, however showing appreciation will test the character of a person. You will soon know!

Showing appreciation is a way for you to show trust in a person. You are trusting that they will not respond by slacking off. People in whom you place trust often become more trustworthy. I believe this is because in showing trust you give them a higher standard of trustworthiness to live up to.

Care for your people

Caring for your people is essential and is key to building trust, though as noted elsewhere, to create trust you need first to have made a commitment to yourself to be trustworthy. Caring is so important that I have devoted a separate detailed section to it.

Ensure your people are properly inducted

When people first join a company, they eagerly seek views from existing employees about what the company is really like and what its culture is. They draw information from any available source, which may include disaffected or resentful employees who see an opportunity to poison a newcomer's attitude. Such opinions carry weight because they're portrayed as what things are really like, rather than the propagandised version that senior management might spout. If a new employee's attitude is poisoned at the outset, it can be very difficult to correct.

To head off this risk it is essential that you get in early and deliver new employees a proper company induction. This has several benefits. Firstly, you can use it to satisfy your legal obligation to instruct people on safety matters and demonstrate how important safety is to your company. Secondly, you can showcase the company's culture. For example, in Chapter 14 I explain why I recommend having the chief executive attend inductions and personally deliver a message of commitment to caring for employees.

In the induction you create a formal setting in which to take the initiative in emphasising those aspects of the company and its culture that are most important to you. The very fact that you talk about culture tells people there is a defined culture, not just some unregulated de facto grouping of default behaviours.

Become good at what you do

People will find it hard to trust you as a leader if you're not good at what you do.
Employees have a lot riding on their leader's ability to manage. People want to work in departments that are well run and well regarded. Put yourself in the position of your people: If as an employee you believe your manager is incompetent, you can't

feel secure working for them, you can't be confident that crises will not develop, that difficult situations will not be mismanaged causing problems for you, and that poor decision-making will not affect you in the long term. You just can't trust your manager.

To be trusted you must be professionally competent. You must have mastery of all the facets of your role. Having mastery of your role allows you to lead and manage proactively. If you do, you are less likely to encounter crises and you are more likely to remain calm, which will benefit you and your people. See the section below on how to cultivate a sense of calm in yourself.

Part of competence is keeping the big picture in view and not getting mired in detail. I also touch on this under the heading of communication. There's never a shortage of detail in our world. Your technical people specialise in detail. You need a grasp of relevant detail, but you must ensure you rise above it and maintain your broad perspective.

Get organised

I have often been complimented and sometimes envied for how well organised I am.

It takes continuous discipline and commitment to be well organised. Fortunately, it becomes a habit and in time you won't need to try so hard as the practice will become hardwired in. You'll reap many benefits, and these will reinforce your well-organised behaviours.

Some leaders and managers are notoriously poorly organised and this makes it difficult for people to trust them even if they are trustworthy in other ways. Poor organisation leads to a person:

▶ not responding to requests in a timely way,

▶ being regarded as a poor communicator,

▶ failing to meet deadlines,

▶ being regarded as unreliable,

▶ being regarded as unhelpful,

▶ being regarded as incompetent,

▶ being seen as lacking transparency — as having something to hide. Others may think you're withholding information when it's just that you were not organised enough to provide it, and

▶ being bypassed — people go around you to someone who gets things done.

Being well organised helps you to keep the commitments you make. If you're well organised, you know what your commitments are and you're likely to have a robust system for keeping track of them. I have an excellent visually based system that never fails me. Knowing what my commitments are and having an effective reminder system allows me to ensure I keep them.

However, 'the best laid plans of mice and men…'. If despite everything you miss a commitment, it's an opportunity to investigate why it happened and to make amends.

Of course, circumstances change and not all commitments can be kept as planned. This presents you with a great opportunity to build trust; if things change and you cannot keep a commitment, as a well-organised person you contact the other party as soon as possible, tell them what happened and together you agree on a new arrangement. Can you think of a time when this didn't happen? For example, have you ever turned up to a scheduled meeting and the other party didn't show, there was no word from them, and you were left hanging? Not a way to engender trust.

Be consultative

Talk to your people and involve them in decision-making where possible. Decisions taken after everyone's input has been obtained are more likely to become embedded and to bring lasting change than ones taken unilaterally and imposed on the majority. What is imposed is opposed.

People feel empowered when you consult them. It is a mark of the value you place on them. They often have valuable contributions to make; why not avail yourself of this input and achieve better results?

These days I'm careful to be consultative, however it was not always the case. In my early years as a manager I believed that rank gave me the right to dictate decisions. Of course, I had responsibility for the decisions I took but the problem was how I reached those decisions. I was not consultative, so too often I missed tapping into the experience and abilities of my people. Being consultative, which I have since learned to do, has had great benefits for me, for my work and for my people.

Here is an example of what can happen when a leader is not consultative. I knew of an information technology manager who had a tendency to push through significant changes like introducing new software without getting input, buy-in and acceptance from the people who would be the primary users of the new resource.

Understandably this led to push-back from those who hadn't been consulted. They were creative in being obstructive; they could be slow to take up the new resource. They could refuse to use it altogether and pretend it didn't exist, merely continuing with the old ways. They could submit endless complaints or change requests and clog up the system. The outcome was that many of these initiatives failed and had to be withdrawn, often after significant cost had been incurred and great time and effort put in by many people.

In response to this ongoing situation and after extensive and broad consultation, a change management program was instituted. The resulting process was simple and effective and didn't add bureaucracy. Consider sponsoring a change management process in your company if you see the need.

A consultative approach is a fundamental aspect of managing change. People fear change; they don't know where it will lead. They don't know whether it will affect their job security. They don't know if they'll be able to deal with it, if they'll be able to understand the new methods or if they'll be humiliated by their inability to cope. Most of these fears are groundless. By consulting your people when contemplating and planning change you can engage them and bring them along with you, solicit their advice and suggestions, help them to understand what the changes will mean then draw out and address their fears. People who have been consulted have no reason to oppose or undermine the change because thanks to you they were involved in bringing it about. You have given them every reason to support it.

It helps if people understand why change is needed. From their perspective the status quo appears just fine and infinitely more desirable than some imagined and feared alternative future. Help your people to understand what has driven the need for change.

As the leader, up to the limits of your authority, you are finally responsible for making decisions. Do not allow yourself to be so mired in consultation that the whole decision-making process gets unduly protracted or grinds to a halt. Define a point at which consultation ceases, you make the decision and arrange for it to be implemented.

Be just and be consistent

Failure to be just and consistent can cause resentment to build up in your people. Helping you to understand resentment is so important that I have devoted a separate chapter to it.

Many of us will have experienced managers who had their favourites in the workforce. These people can do no wrong. Others strive to do their best and receive little recognition while the favourite does less and receives more praise and attention. They often have the manager's ear and their opinion is heeded whether valid or not.

When we see this, our sense of justice is offended. We feel resentment that is fuelled every time we observe the manager's behaviour and this may be every working day. We perceive the manager as acting unjustly and inconsistently. It's difficult to trust a person whom we perceive as inconsistent because their behaviour is unpredictable. A given achievement such as a task performed well should receive its reward justly and consistently across the workgroup.

Quite apart from the barrier it puts up to trust, unjust and inconsistent behaviour demotivates and demoralises. The message it sends is: 'no matter what I do, no matter how hard I try, I may not receive a just reward or any reward.' The just reward may be no more than a thank-you for your efforts but when given, it's enough to satisfy the individual and reinforce the actions.

Not long before I started with a new employer, one of the crane operators had been issued a written warning. The reason was that he drove his crane up to the out gate on a client site and handed his ID swipe card to his rigger (travelling with him in the crane) who disembarked and swiped out for him. The offence was that he had not swiped out personally. I sensed something amiss. When I investigated, I found that from the cab of the crane the operator could not reach the swipe card reader because it was too low. There was no place to park his crane at the gate. He could not drive his crane out to the parking area until he had swiped out. So he was stuck. I also found that the practice of crane operators handing their swipe cards to their riggers to swipe out was widespread for the above reasons and that the written warning had been issued to placate the client. So as the written warning was manifestly unjust, I revoked it and informed the crane operator and the client.

Practise humility

> *The proud man can learn humility,*
> *but he will be proud of it.*
> – **Mignon McLaughlin.**

> *If I only had a little humility, I'd be perfect.*
> – **Ted Turner.**

Humility is the quality of being modest or respectful. It translates to treating people as equals and valuing them and their input unconditionally. Humility in its various forms is widely seen as a virtue in many religious and philosophical traditions, being connected with notions of egoless-ness.

In some companies the chief executive and senior managers swagger about with perceptible sneers, manifesting their sense of superiority over the mass of the employees. If it's not apparent in their facial expression, you can see it in their body language. Is your company like that? Are you like that? These are rhetorical questions but they're also an opportunity for you to do a reality check.

People appreciate me for my humility. I treat my people as equals and I seek out, value and recognise their contribution. It wasn't always so. In my earlier days, my nickname among some of the Australian mine tyre service people was "Hitler". So things certainly changed!

A humble leader says in effect: 'I may be senior to you in rank but I acknowledge that as human beings we are equal. I may be better at some things than you are, but I know you're better at other things than I am. I will treat you as my equal in human terms.'

The appreciation people have for humility has been shown to me in an unexpected way — what people have written on my farewell cards when I was leaving various roles. Your people may not mention your humility when you're there day-to-day, but when you're leaving they take the opportunity to think about their true feelings and express them.

Humility recognises that rank does not determine power. It may determine authority but leaders who wield power based on their rank are likely to create resentment that can fester and surface as resistance in various forms (see Chapter 10).

So in practical terms, how do you demonstrate humility?

▶ Be consultative. By doing this you demonstrate your appreciation for the contribution of others and show that you value them.

▶ Make amends when you have wronged someone. This shows that you are prepared to hold yourself accountable for your actions including mistakes (see Chapter 12).

▶ Take every opportunity to show how much you value people. Cultivate an attitude of gratitude. See the separate section on this with stories from my past.

Another perspective on humility is how you think of your place in the organisation chart for your department or team. Typically, managers think of themselves as being at the top of their particular pyramid; this is the way organisation charts are drawn with the most senior people at the top and others in descending rank order below them. Why not flip this view? Why not think of yourself as being at the bottom of the pyramid, supporting all those who are doing the work? In a very real sense this is where you are. You are still the leader but you are leading by facilitating the removal of obstacles so your people can do their jobs unhindered.

In my experience most employees want to do their best, but they can be prevented from doing so by a build-up of frustration. If people meet frustration at every turn, they eventually give up or at least try less hard. The frustrations I'm referring to are things like managers who micro-manage, a culture of blame, a lack of proper systems and processes and a lack of clarity about who is responsible for what. As a leader you should make it your mission to eliminate these and other sources of frustration so your people are not demotivated and can perform at their best.

There is a view that leaders should only ever be at the front, or in the case of the organisation chart, at the top. This may have come from the military model — for example, officers being the first to "go over the top" during assaults from the trenches in World War I. At times as a leader, you'll certainly need to be at the front but much of the time your role can be supporting your people and ensuring they have what they need to do their jobs.

To be a manager and a leader you need to have strong self-belief. So is humility at odds with strong self-belief? I think not. With strong self-belief you have a sense of power coming from within. You are confident; you don't need to compensate by being overly assertive. And you can be humble.

Look after your and your people's physical health

If you are physically fit, compared to those who are less so you will have more physical and mental energy and be more productive and creative. Your risk of getting many diseases will be reduced. As a leader, by engaging in fitness activities you model fitness for your people; this leads them to become more motivated to keep fit and as they do, they will derive the above benefits as well.

In addition to modelling fitness and encouraging exercise it's important to create opportunities for your people to exercise. One of my managers, the owner of the company, was a keen runner. Our office was located near a beautiful park situated along a river, so at lunchtimes he would run along the river and up through the park back to the office. He encouraged the rest of us to do the same. He had a shower room installed in the building. Many of us took a lunchtime run and I am convinced it brought significant benefits to our health and productivity as well as to our enjoyment of work.

Look after your and your people's mental health

Part of what allows you to be trusted by those around and under you is behaving toward them in a consistent, rational and calm manner. If you are to do this, you need to take care of your mental health.

By mental health I am referring to your state of mind, as it is most of the time. Mental health issues exist across a spectrum. They range from so mild that the sufferer is barely aware of them to so serious that the individual is unable to function and requires medical intervention. We all have times when we're downcast or anxious about problems or about our future. But if these times grow to dominate most of our waking hours, we need to take action.

Mental health problems such as depression and anxiety have become widespread in Western society. They can be very debilitating, psychologically paralysing, can seriously impair your ability to function as a leader and manager and can damage your relationships.

Mental health problems are treatable and manageable. You don't need to bear these burdens for the rest of your days.

When I reached my mid-thirties, I became aware of how

much personal "baggage" I was carrying. When I refer to baggage I'm talking about the lingering regrets from past negative experiences. Causes included ongoing problems in relations with my parents, relationships that had failed or ended prematurely, difficulties at work, inability to get on with certain people, financial pressures, etc. I'm sure you could write your own list.

All of this had its effect on me. I was becoming increasingly short-tempered. I noticed that certain situations triggered this anger and the anger was almost always unproductive and destructive of relationships. My temper was ruining my life. If you notice that certain situations always trigger certain negative responses in you, that is reason to explore what is behind the triggers.

I also noticed a gradual build-up in my internal self-talk — the conversations taking place inside my head. This happened over a period of years, so slowly that for a long time I didn't notice the change. Gradual changes are always more difficult to spot. It was so much a part of me that I regarded it as normal. And it was — up to a point. When I woke up to how pervasive it was and found I could not rid myself of it and find peace of mind, I realised it had become abnormal.

Everything reached a climax when I was in my late thirties and I had to seek help. I have since worked hard to maintain and improve my mental health and this work is ongoing.

I've thought a lot about why these issues came to a head when they did. My conclusions are expressed in the following graph. Time in years is on the horizontal axis with recent years on the right. On the vertical axis, higher means more.

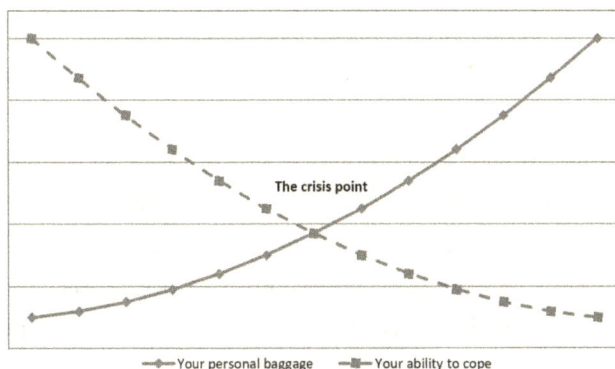

The crisis point

——◆—— Your personal baggage   ——■—— Your ability to cope

As I see it, unless you take action to rid yourself of personal baggage it builds up over the years for the reasons listed above and for other reasons particular to you. This baggage consists of a mixture of regrets, guilt, sadness, feelings of inadequacy because you couldn't make things turn out as you wanted, and resentment toward others for their actions. The solid line on the graph depicts this.

In your earlier years you may be oblivious to these feelings as you are more naturally resilient and able to cast them aside with relative ease; in fact, you may not even realise you're doing it. As time passes you become less resilient, things affect you more and your ability to cope diminishes. The dashed line on the graph shows this. Unless you deal with your baggage, at some point it reaches the same level as your diminishing ability to cope. The curves intersect and cross and this may precipitate a crisis in your life. This happened to me and I have seen many people experience life crises that I attribute to this.

Resilience is your ability to bounce back from adversity to a normal state or simply not be affected by adversity. We all need resilience because not everything that happens in our lives is positive. Research has shown that resilience is influenced by the ratio of positive to negative experiences we have; like a boxer we can be floored by a succession of hard blows but equally if we experience predominantly positive experiences our resilience improves. So it's important to ensure that you are happy and fulfilled in your work and your relationships.

To build resilience, among other things we need to seek out environments and situations where we are likely to have many more positive experiences than negative ones. There is a connection here to what you spend your days doing. You're likely to have more positive experiences if you enjoy your work and if it's meaningful to you. So do you love your work? Or do you drag your sorry backside into the office each day longing for the time when you can go home? If the latter, you should consider seeking fulfilment elsewhere and pursuing your dreams.

There is also a link between the amount of baggage you're carrying and your level of resilience. The more baggage you have, the less resilient you're likely to be. You may be crushed by what has happened to you and unable to dig yourself out from under it.

If you work on reducing the baggage you're carrying and on increasing your resilience and your ability to cope with life's challenges, the curves never cross and you never reach a point of crisis. This is illustrated in the graph below.

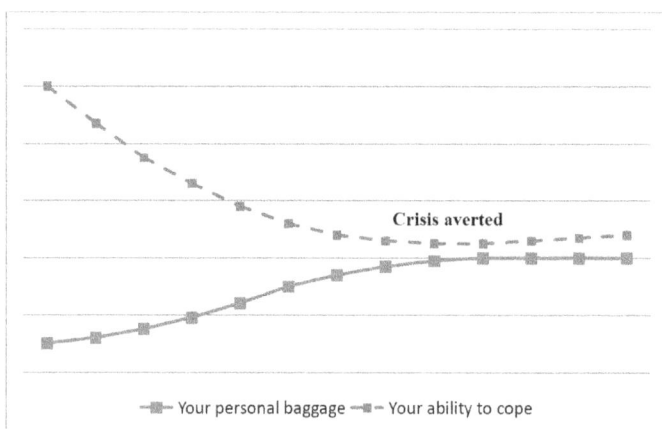

Crisis averted

Your personal baggage — Your ability to cope

So to return to my own story, I began work on my mental health. I started by seeking counselling. My first counsellor was Annette M. who taught me re-birthing and Conscious Connected Breathing. I'm grateful to Annette; she showed me a path to a better life and I've been on that path ever since. One benefit of counselling is that it allows you to gain a better understanding of why certain things happened to you and what your role was in them.

I didn't just rely on counselling. I undertook many self-help activities. One book that I found particularly helpful was John Gray's "How to Get What You Want and Want What You Have". It has some excellent techniques that I've used to good effect and I highly recommend it.

My belief is that the lingering effect of past negative events can keep a hold over us and influence our behaviour years later by lurking unseen in the darkest recesses of our mind and surfacing as destructive behaviour when triggered. We need to deal with these influences so they no longer have power over us. Believe me when I say that once you do so, life becomes much more peaceful, enjoyable and productive.

Let's talk for a moment about onions. The property of onions we're interested in is their soft concentric layers each of which can be peeled away to reveal the next, and the way a freshly exposed layer gradually hardens when exposed to the air.

Imagine peeling off the hard outer husk of an onion to reveal the first moist layer then leaving the onion on the bench. Exposed to air this layer gradually dries and toughens. Then visualise after a few days peeling off this newly hardened layer to expose the next layer and replacing the now-smaller onion on the bench. Imagine this process being repeated. Eventually you reach a point where there are no more layers to remove and you have reached the core.

We humans all have an outer layer that can be quite tough, protecting us from our principal vulnerability. Our deeper-lying vulnerabilities are also shielded.

This outer layer is not impregnable. It can break down when we are exposed to triggers related to a specific vulnerability that the outer layer is protecting us against. We may think we have mastery over ourselves; it's only when we are exposed to a trigger that we realise we don't. Years may pass between triggering events. Our response to triggers can be quite extreme. Because our defences have been breached unexpectedly, we're not prepared and we don't have control of ourselves. We are in uncharted territory.

Rather than rely on protective layers it's better to deal with your issues so you no longer need protection from them. Also, you expend energy maintaining your protective layer and suppressing the responses that want to break through. This energy is unproductive. It's like having a wall around your property to keep out intruders, a wall that stays up only if you keep holding it up. If your protective layers were not needed, the energy used to maintain them could be put to far better use, for example helping you to become calmer and grow your creativity, spontaneity and desire to engage. It's like moving to a better neighbourhood where you no longer need a wall.

Dealing with a past issue removes the need for that protective layer and allows you to peel it away. In doing so you expose the next issue. You may feel vulnerable until you deal with that issue. Expect to feel relief each time you deal with an issue.

Some issues are deeply buried. My experience was that as I dealt with issues and peeled away layers I gradually exposed layers I didn't even know existed. For example, at elementary school I was bullied and threatened by my best friend — or so I thought he was — which affected me badly at the time. I never spoke of it and if I thought about it, which was rare, it was as a far-off event. However, as an adult, during the process of peeling my personal onion, it came back to me forcefully and very emotionally and I realised that I had merely been keeping a lid on it for all those years. Once I understood that it still had a hold over me, I was able to set about dealing with it. I did that and now I can talk about it without emotion. We cannot always sense the deeper issues until we've dealt with the ones that are more apparent to us.

So how long do you need to continue the process of dealing with your issues? Continue until there are no more issues or at least no more that are significant to you. You may choose to deal with several issues then take a break before the next round. Or you may have only a handful of issues that require attention and find that you can comfortably deal with them all in quick succession.

As you deal with each issue it may take time before other issues surface. Allow whatever time you need. If you were renovating your home, you wouldn't try to complete it over a weekend.

Do you ever get to a final layer or to the core? I don't know — I'm not there yet. But I'm definitely on the way.

I continue to work on my mental health. At various times I've suffered job loss, been unemployed, nearly lost my home due to joblessness and lack of income, suffered from bouts of depression including one short period when I was suicidal, and survived cancer. However here I am, stronger than ever and with an understanding of these issues that I can pass on to help you avoid or minimise the pitfalls.

As you peel each layer away you get closer to the real you that lies within — the person that no longer needs the protection of those layers. I believe this has been the most valuable thing for me. I feel as if it is now a truer me that I project. From what you've read of this book so far, you would understand that an authentic you is easier for people to trust.

You can build trust by working to protect and enhance your people's mental health. This is also a way of showing care. When you understand the factors that influence your own mental health you can see how these and similar factors can impact the mental health of others.

The first step to helping others with their mental health is to monitor how they're doing day-to-day. This should be part of your everyday interaction with them. As you talk with people you look for signs that anything has changed or that all is not well. For example, if you're talking to someone who is normally outgoing and you see they're unusually quiet and withdrawn, make a mental note. Everyone has periods of reflection but if the uncharacteristic behaviour persists you should act. Take the person aside and ask them if anything is wrong. This is a caring act. People carrying a burden are often happy to talk it out with someone they trust. A burden shared is a burden halved. Talking through it will help to clarify it for them. Then the person may know what needs to be done. After hearing what they have to say you may have helpful suggestions.

Referring people in need to your company's Employee Assistance Program (EAP — free anonymous counselling often provided by employers for their employees) is a good way to get them started on a path to better mental health. The benefits of EAPs are covered in detail in another section.

Cultivate a sense of calm in yourself

People appreciate being around people who are calm.

Calmness in a leader provides great reassurance especially in times of stress. A calm leader inspires people. By being calm you can help those around you to remain calm — a better state for them and for you.

Imagine if an airliner you were travelling on developed a problem, the captain addressed the passengers over the PA system and you could hear the agitation in his voice.

Most of the time I'm very calm. I receive compliments about this especially from people who've been led by others who are easily agitated and generally not calm.

It's easy enough to be stressed during the working day — there are certainly enough pressures. Trying to stay on top of your emails will do it!

A state of calm is more difficult to maintain if you manage reactively, if you just wait for crises to erupt and only then do you spring into action. For those who manage this way there will be plenty of crises. Such people look busy and this may be appealing to their superiors. However, all that busyness comes at a cost, usually in the form of poorly managed outcomes and stressed people around them. Leaders who are proactive have a much better chance of remaining calm because they experience fewer crises.

I once said to a person I had just promoted to manager that within two years I wanted to see him with his feet up on his desk for a part of each day. While the comment was tongue-in-cheek, my message was that if he was managing properly there would be very few crises in his area and he would have time to think and plan.

Make a conscious decision to cultivate calm. Teach yourself to be aware of what causes you to become stressed then do whatever is necessary to lower your stress level. This may be nothing more than a walk to the lunchroom to grab a glass of water, a few deep breaths and a couple of minutes putting the stressful situation into its proper perspective. Remember that if you were to disappear in a puff of smoke the company would find a way to cope without you. Few stressors truly deserve the level of stress they create.

The ability to stay calm in your work is a good barometer. If you're unable to remain calm, take a step back and identify what is stressing you and keeping you from being calm. Are you insecure about your ability to perform the role? Do you need more training? Are you getting enough support from your manager? Is there unresolved conflict around you? Would you benefit from being mentored? Is the role a good fit for your skills, qualifications and experience? Is the role in line with your aspirations? Are you passionate about it? You'll need to be honest about all this, then have the strength to take action to put it right.

Of course, stressors at home can carry across to the workplace and vice-versa.

Consider taking up meditation to promote a state of calm. Wikipedia has this to say about meditation: "Meditation refers to a broad variety of practices that include techniques designed to promote relaxation, build internal energy or life force and develop compassion, love, patience, generosity and forgiveness. Meditation has a calming effect and directs awareness inward until pure awareness is achieved, described as 'being awake inside without being aware of anything except awareness itself'." Meditation need not have a religious or spiritual flavour. I believe we all need a practical meditation technique in our toolkit, and we should practise meditation on a regular basis, preferably daily.

My first experience of meditation was when I was in my early twenties. Later I learned a powerful form of meditation known as Conscious Connected Breathing as I mentioned previously. I have since used a number of meditation techniques and I have come to regard meditation as an essential part of leading a calm life. Apart from all the other benefits I feel better and I sleep better when I meditate regularly.

Take up meditation and encourage your people to do it as well.

I mention meditation because of the influence I know it has over my ability to remain calm. I actively cultivate a sense of calm and this is infectious in a positive way. I talk to others about my commitment to remaining calm, to show them that there is a practical alternative to leading a life of agitation and stress.

Give people your undivided attention and listen actively

A good way to validate people and to ensure the best quality of communication is to give them your undivided attention when talking with them, especially face-to-face.

This is not easy especially in high-pressure or noisy situations. You may have a mobile phone with you and a two-way radio. Your team may expect you to be available at all times to resolve problems. There may be unpredictable noise (you must always protect your hearing; what I'm referring to here is noise sufficient to interfere with a conversation without being above legal limits).

Let's use the example of a member of your team who approaches you wanting to discuss something.

You don't know how significant a conversation will be until you've had it. So create an environment where the communication will be high quality. If the matter is urgent, you'll probably need to deal with it then and there irrespective of circumstances. However, many important matters are not to-the-minute urgent. If the immediate environment is not conducive to good communication (for example, a lot of noise or a high likelihood of interruption) tell the person you are keen to make sure you hear what they have to say and ask if the conversation can be held somewhere quieter.

If the conversation has to be deferred, try to avoid deferring it by more than an hour or so. The other person needs to know you are not trying to avoid having the conversation. An hour's delay or less minimises the risk of this perception.

When you're conversing, practise giving people your undivided attention. They will appreciate it. It's not easy. There are many distractions waiting to crowd in: your thoughts such as concern over the state of your email inbox, that intractable problem in Maintenance that's affecting your department, the urgent request from Finance for the figures. Learn to block out these distractions.

Face the other person with an open stance, head slightly forward, maintaining eye contact. Nod as you listen to what they say.

Let the other person finish speaking. Often people provide the context first and deliver the important information at the end. If you jump in early, you'll cut them off and may miss out on the most important part.

Focus on what the person is saying rather than on preparing your response. It's tempting to be mentally drafting your reply rather than listening, especially if you disagree with the other person's point of view. If you do, you're likely to miss the most important part of what they're saying. Also, if you're doing this it is normally apparent to the other party. We've all seen it; the listener's face clouds over, their eyes drift off and we can tell they're getting their response ready and no longer listening to us.

For critical situations, restate in your own words what you believe the other person said; this allows them to check that you've understood. This was a technique I developed and used when I lived in Chile. Most people I dealt with spoke only Spanish; in my early days there when my understanding of Spanish wasn't the best, this technique assured me and the other party that I had taken the correct meaning from their words.

If a person has a sensitive subject to discuss they will be looking for clues as to how receptive you are. If you look disinterested or your body language conveys this they may not pass on the vital information.

At the end of the conversation, thank the other person. They may have done you a big favour with what they've told you.

Monitor your body language

What you say when you speak and what you say with your body can be very different. If there is a disconnect between them, people will notice. It will ring alarm bells with them and impair their ability to trust you.

For example, let's say you invite Christine in to discuss a personal concern she has raised. She comes in and you both sit down, preferably adjacent rather than separated by a desk or table. As the conversation starts you appear to be listening, but your legs are crossed pointing away from her, your arms are folded across your chest and you have a sceptical frown on your face.

What will the effect be? The lack of congruence between your declared interest in what she is saying and what your body is communicating is likely to cause Christine to doubt your sincerity. She may only pick up these cues subconsciously, but it will lead to a loss of trust that may have repercussions for your working relationship with her. The immediate effect is likely to be that Christine will withhold the most sensitive and important information she had planned to share with you. This will prevent you from helping to resolve the issue that is troubling her and will create a barrier between you. It may also deny you access to important information you need. She may be reluctant to approach you in future.

Your body language also impacts the other person's perceptions of whether you are giving them your undivided attention.

Make an effort to learn at least the basics of body language so you understand what your and other people's body language is saying. Monitor your own body language to ensure it aligns with what you're saying. If it won't be tamed, ask yourself if this is revealing thoughts or attitudes about the subject or the other person that you need to acknowledge and act on.

Be aware of the effect your mood has on others

In my early days as a manager I would sometimes come to work in a mood. This was not usually a bad mood although at times it could be; most of the time it was just that I was keeping to myself, being more reflective or introspective than normal.

I began to notice that my mood affected my workforce. If

I came in feeling extroverted and on top of the world then all was well. My people mirrored that. If I came in feeling withdrawn or in a low mood, within an hour my people's mood would have sunk as well.

It's not fair to impose your negative moods on your people. As a leader, monitor your mood as you travel to work and resolve to leave any negative feelings at the door.

Watch your email etiquette

There are some simple rules about emailing that will help you build trust and avoid creating resentment.

Email is great for controlling the content of your message and not being side-tracked by the recipient's reactions as can happen with direct personal contact. It's very useful for confirming to another person your understanding of what was said or agreed and recording it for posterity. Email is not so good for resolving disputes and definitely not good for giving criticism. Consider the following when emailing:

- ► Apply the four Cs: complete, clear, correct and conversational.

- ► Stay brief. Most people already get too many emails and too much content.

- ► Ensure before you email that it is the most appropriate way to communicate with that person at that time.

- ► If face-to-face is what's needed, do that instead

of emailing. If face-to-face is not possible, make a phone call in preference to emailing.

▶ Assume that an email you send may end up anywhere and frame it accordingly.

▶ Avoid criticising by email. If you believe criticism is called for, it's best to do it in person or by phone if that's the only other option.

▶ Humour in emails may fall flat or be misinterpreted. Keep it for people you know well!

To help keep your inbox under control you can apply the four Ds as well: do, delegate, defer or delete.

Become good at communicating

How is good communication linked to trust?

For a person to trust you, to some degree they must get inside you to know what's there. One way they do that is by observing how you communicate with them. If you communicate clearly, people will take it that you have nothing to hide. Clarity fosters trust.

Leonardo Da Vinci is quoted as saying 'simplicity is the ultimate sophistication'. For our purposes, he meant that if you have mastery of a complex subject you can break it down into simple chunks that others can understand.

Most subjects have an underlying simplicity that you must strive to find. Even a detailed and complex subject can be laid out in a structured series of simple statements, each building on the previous one to create the full picture. I believe people inherently understand the truth of this even if they can't always do it themselves.

In our world there's no shortage of detail, in fact increasingly there's too much. But the fundamental truth of any situation is still there, just a bit more deeply buried and harder to dig out.

Imagine a person you're getting to know and whom you find communicates in a needlessly complex and roundabout way. If I'm on the receiving end my first reaction will be that they're not too clever, that they're incapable of cutting through the detail to extract what's important so they can convey it, or that they confuse providing a mass of information with communicating clearly. I may also be a bit peeved that they're wasting my time because it becomes my challenge to unpack what they've said, pull out the important bits and repack them in logical order.

If my other evidence about the person is that they're not intellectually challenged and not known as a poor communicator my next thought may be that they have an agenda: that perhaps they don't really want me to understand. I have encountered this a couple of times in my career.

Like all busy people I want to receive information in the most efficient way, and I have limited tolerance for people who don't deliver it that way.

It's not unknown for people to hoard information of which they are custodians, so they retain power over others. One way to achieve this is to communicate so poorly that the information appears beyond reach. In truth very little information is beyond reach if properly communicated. If you are listening to a so-called expert and you can't understand what they're saying, blame them, not yourself.

I had the experience of joining a company in a senior role where I was responsible for several departments including industrial relations with which I was relatively unfamiliar. Another senior manager had responsibility for this area, and it was planned that as part of the restructure he would hand it over to me, which he said he was happy to do. He gave me several briefings that I found totally incomprehensible and impenetrable and I resolved to learn about it without his "help". I came to believe that he didn't really want to hand over the portfolio because in his mind to do so would diminish his value to the company, so he was trying to obstruct my learning.

In another managerial role I had an admin person reporting to me. Soon after I took up my role, this mature age lady resigned because her husband had been transferred to another part of the country. I had to move quickly to recruit and train a replacement. I asked the incumbent for a copy of the procedures for her job and was shocked to find there were none — each person was just trained verbally and carried the procedures in their head.

In short order I found a replacement person — a teenager who was working as a checkout supervisor at the local supermarket. She came to my notice because she was by far the youngest checkout supervisor there, so she clearly had ability and potential.

The incumbent set about training her. Initially I just observed as the older lady trained the new recruit. I saw that the training consisted of the older lady spouting procedures as fast as she could, so fast that no reasonable person could understand or absorb them. So I ended up standing behind both women with my digital recorder taking down what was said then transcribing it later to create a procedures manual for the job. It turned out that the older lady was behaving this way because she felt demeaned that I had replaced her with a young and inexperienced person.

So how does all this relate to trust? Would you trust a person who purports to be communicating transparently with you when actually they're not?

A related problem occurs when someone provides you with information that later proves to be wholly or partly untrue. You would naturally investigate whether this came about by accident or by intent. If the latter, you would lose trust in the person and you may struggle to regain it.

Good communication requires skills that must be learned and practised. It starts with clear thinking. This does not come naturally to everyone. Clear thinking is fundamental to clear communication; clear communication always consists of logically structured delivery of material and that is possible only when you have thought clearly about it.

You may have to train and mentor your people to think and communicate clearly.

So what can we as managers and leaders do? Firstly, strive to communicate clearly at all times. Secondly, strive to structure our arguments logically. Thirdly, cultivate our ability to speak in public. I now consider each of these.

Strive to communicate clearly

Start by committing yourself to communicate clearly and not to tolerate unclear communication from others. Improve your communication skills by learning from others whom you regard as clear communicators. Ask them how they achieve it. Ask one of them to become your mentor with a focus on communication.

Have you ever admired a painting but felt that something was not quite right about it? If so, what you're usually noticing is that the perspective — the representation of three-dimensional objects on a two-dimensional surface — is off. We may not know much about perspective, but we can tell when it's not right.

Equally, we can often tell if a document is poorly structured; the facts don't appear in the right order and this makes the document difficult to read and understand.

If people are drafting documents for you, make sure what they write is logically structured, clear, concise and free from excess verbiage. If it's not, politely send it back to be fixed. Offer to work with the drafter to show them what you want. Concentrate first on the structure and the order in which important facts are conveyed; if these are not right the document can never be right. As you review the draft you can evaluate how clearly the writer was thinking. You'll be doing the drafter a big favour by making clear what standard you expect. They'll probably do better next time!

Develop your structure logically

If you're thinking of building a brick wall, you understand that first a foundation must be laid then the courses of bricks are laid one course at a time. You wouldn't consider laying the upper courses before the foundation because physically it couldn't be done. Yet when people communicate, they're not subject to these constraints. So much communication takes place without a proper foundation. I have often found myself mentally rearranging someone's presentation or material into the proper order.

Here's the process I use and recommend for bringing

structure to your longer written communications and your presentations.

- ▶ Assemble all the relevant facts. Use brainstorming if appropriate. Gather ideas in the order in which they come to you. Type them into a Word document, one item per line with a space between each line. The order of the points doesn't matter as you will assemble them into a logical sequence later.

- ▶ Put the document away for a day or so.

- ▶ Pull it back out and review it. You'll approach it with a fresh perspective. You may come up with additional points.

- ▶ Review what you've written and identify the fundamentals of what you're trying to express.

- ▶ Re-order your points into a logical sequence that starts with the foundational material then moves on to the higher-order facts.

- ▶ You may well see that bits are missing. Go looking for them and insert them where they belong.

- ▶ Put the document away for a day or so.

- ▶ Come back to it again and repeat the process.

- ▶ When you're happy with the document, ask another person to check that it makes sense and is complete.

This is an iterative process. The order in which information should be presented and what should be included or left out is often not immediately apparent. So much of developing a clear communication such as a report or presentation is based on your subconscious mind processing information you've assembled, when you're not consciously working on it. It takes time, so don't leave it to the last minute!

Cultivate your ability to speak in public

Being able to speak well in public is an essential skill for any leader. "Public" ranges from just a handful of people at a meeting up to hundreds of delegates at a conference.

My first public speech was not a success. It was the occasion of my year twelve graduation dinner and I had been chosen to make the speech on behalf of the boys. I remember it well. Just into my speech I froze. My vision went blurry, my heart was pounding, it was as if I had entered a parallel universe where everyone could still see and hear me but in which I had been turned to stone. The girl who was to make the other speech saw what was happening and saved me by jumping in and starting her speech early. For me it was mortifying experience and an inauspicious start to the large amount of public speaking I have since done.

Over time I analysed what had gone wrong. Firstly, I had done insufficient preparation, believing I could wing it. I could wing it now but these days I'm an experienced speaker. Even so, now I always have a backup plan. Secondly, I had not made notes of the topics I wanted to cover; a handful of points written on a small card would have been enough so that if I got lost I could refer to it and reorient myself.

Normally if I am making a presentation, I support it with PowerPoint slides. I find it useful to have something for the audience to focus on without having so much on the screen that they get caught up reading it and don't hear what I'm saying. There are alternatives to PowerPoint that you should explore however PowerPoint is a good place to start.

PowerPoint is also valuable when you're drafting a presentation. You can use it to list and develop your bullet points.

Ensure whatever goes up on the screen has some image content, not just words.

Here is what works well for me in public speaking. I am assuming that you plan to support your presentation with visuals of some kind.

- ▶ Ensure what you plan to say meets the standards of logic and structure that I have outlined.

- ▶ Place no more than six bullet points on each slide as memory aids for what you wish to expand on. Don't just read the points out. It's boring and belittling for the audience if you only read from your slides. They could do that themselves and you might just as well give them a copy of the presentation and walk away; you're not adding value. As a speaker you have the opportunity to convey your passion for the topic and leave the audience with a strong message about what is important to you. You can achieve this only if you use the presentation as a foundation and add to it as you deliver.

- ▶ Be fully familiar with your subject matter. If you're not, go back and do more work before you deliver.

▶ Practise a lot before you present. If you're well practised, you'll feel more confident and be less likely to
panic. Before a presentation I had to give to 400 delegates at a safety conference, I created and refined
the PowerPoint slides then practised the whole half
hour's worth in my home office more than twenty
times. I felt very confident of my material and my
ability to deliver it compellingly within the allot-
ted time, as indeed I did. This is in line with the
principle of performance: amateurs practise until
they get it right; professionals practise until they
can't get it wrong.

▶ Feeling nervous before a presentation is normal but
is not helpful if it threatens to overwhelm you. You
may feel your heart banging away and that adds
to your stress. My trick is that on the way to the
podium I take a few deep breaths and hold each one
for two or three seconds before exhaling. Any longer and you may feel faint. The extra oxygenation
your blood gets from each held breath reduces your
pulse rate and this relaxes you. It certainly works
for me.

▶ Bring two digital copies of your presentation on separate memory sticks or other portable media in case
the copy you emailed to the organisers doesn't work.

▶ Bring a hard copy of your slides and have this with
you at the podium. On one occasion when I was delivering a presentation to seventy mining executives, the
audio-visuals failed completely. I was unruffled and

continued seamlessly with the presentation because I had the hard copy available. However, I have seen it go badly; I attended another presentation where the audio-visuals failed. The presenter was totally flummoxed and his presentation fell apart.

Encourage people to bring you the bad news

We're all familiar with Hans Christian Andersen's tale "The Emperor's New Clothes". It tells of a vain emperor for whom two swindlers fashioned a suit of clothes that would be invisible to all except those who were worthy of their positions. Of course the suit didn't actually exist and the emperor was strutting about in the altogether. His courtiers dared not expose the deception for fear of being deemed unworthy. In the end it took an innocent child to point out that the emperor was naked.

Although this was a fable, one sees it play out in business. Some people in senior roles cannot bear bad news, so people stop bringing it to them. The truth eventually emerges but by then it's too late to manage the situation well.

Bad news is the most valuable news we can have. Who wants to receive just the good news if there is bad news out there too? When bad news is delivered promptly it provides an opportunity to make a measured response.

Employees are typically aware of bad news and know it must be confronted and dealt with. But if the leader lacks the stomach to do it, people lose trust.

Part of a leader's role is to protect their people and relieve them of stress. In part they do this by giving people confidence that they will handle difficult issues competently. A leader who is unable or unwilling to do this and expresses it by showing dislike for receiving bad news cannot and will not be trusted.

Exercises

→ Practise making and keeping commitments however small.

→ Have you ever been guilty of letting a safety breach go unreported so that operations would not be interrupted? What happened? Were you exposed? How was your credibility affected?

→ Review your conduct against the ethics checklist above. How do you score?

→ How do you handle information that pops up on the grapevine?

→ How many times a week do you show appreciation for your people?

→ How good is the induction in your company? How could you improve it?

→ How good are you at your job? Is it a good fit for you? Is it what you're passionate about?

Exercises (continued)

→ How do you rate your level of organisation on a scale from one to ten?

→ Are you known as consultative?

→ Have you ever rescinded a penalty because you found it was unjust?

→ Would your people describe you as humble?

→ How would you describe your mental health?

→ Do you remain calm in difficult situations?

→ Are you known for giving people your undivided attention and listening actively?

→ How do you rate your communication skills?

→ How good are you at public speaking?

Chapter 7

Trust and empower your people

He who mistrusts most should be trusted least.
– Theognis of Megara, Greek poet.

So far we've talked about how to become a person whom others trust, however trust cuts both ways. You could be the most trustworthy person but if you do not trust and empower your people, the trust they can extend to you will be limited.

In part there is a natural *quid pro quo* stemming from people's sense of justice. People believe that if they are to trust you, you should trust them.

Competent and well-trained people rightly believe that they should be trusted to do tasks without excessive monitoring.

A person who is trustworthy and to whom trustworthiness is important will deeply resent not being trusted.

Trust and empowerment go hand in hand. If you trust a person, it follows that you should empower them — free them to do tasks within their capability and the limits of their authority without undue scrutiny from you.

What are the benefits of having empowered people working for you? They get on with the job quietly and productively. They don't pester you for support. They contact you when they need help or when they run out of tasks and want more. This is separate from your routine interactions with them that are likely to be pleasant on both sides. They're happy doing what they're doing and you're happy with them.

How to empower your people and show trust

Train people properly

You cannot reasonably set a person to perform a task if they're not adequately trained. So identify and provide the required training then follow up to ensure that it has been absorbed and understood and is being applied.

If formal training is required, provide it. Then monitor the trainee on a regular basis to ensure they're practising what they've learned so it becomes embedded.

Teaching people to fly taught me a lot about how people learn and how to guide their progress. Let's say I was planning to teach a student a new flight manoeuvre. So they could absorb information more easily, I would first brief them on the ground rather than in the pressure-cooker environment up in the air. I would then take the student up. Once in flight I would demonstrate the new manoeuvre, let the student perform it then critique their performance, explaining to them what went wrong and how to fix it. I would then ask the student to perform the manoeuvre again and critique the second attempt. We would then repeat the whole process until the student was competent to practise the manoeuvre. After the student had practised the manoeuvre solo a few times, I would review them to ensure they hadn't picked up bad habits.

How I critiqued the student's performance in flight between manoeuvres was crucial. During a flying lesson the student is normally on the point of overload so they cannot absorb lengthy critiques. I found that I had about thirty seconds between manoeuvres to explain to the student what, if anything, had gone wrong with their execution and advise them how to fix it. Any longer and they could not absorb what I was saying.

This sequence works for training people in a non-flying environment as well. It's preferable to start with a written procedure for the activity and to allow the trainee time to become familiar with it. A competent person should explain the procedure and take the trainee through the activity. Then the trainee performs it and the trainer constructively critiques their performance. When the activity has been mastered the trainee can go solo. You should also provide access to ongoing support as discussed below.

Some people need more training than others. Some pick things up quickly; others take longer. That is not to say the slower ones are inferior though they may need more effort on the trainer's part and on their part to reach the required standard. Once they have, they can be as good as the faster learners.

Doing new tasks should be a success experience for people so they enjoy their work and their sense of confidence and empowerment grows. As the leader you need to set things up to ensure this happens. Again this is a trust issue. Your people entrust you with managing their training so they can cope as they go along. Be ready with the spanner but don't take the trainer wheels off too soon.

Of course, each individual must play their part in ensuring they obtain appropriate training as part of their career progression. What I'm referring to here is ensuring people are appropriately trained and supported in the tasks they are required to perform.

Set up post training support

Irrespective of how quickly people learn, they need to be supported after they've been trained. This is best done on a structured basis so that the trainer or a nominated experienced person has a pre-arranged session with them initially every few days. Later the interval can be extended. This way the trainees don't need to be the ones initiating trainer contact which some may be reluctant to do. However, make sure the trainee has access to a trainer whenever needed so they can resolve the inevitable questions without having to wait for a scheduled session.

Avoid micro-managing

Micromanagement refers to a way of managing where the manager, literally or figuratively, stands behind the employee and dictates the minutiae of their work.

Many of you will have experienced being micromanaged. It's infuriating. It's demeaning. It's disempowering. It destroys trust.

Do you micromanage your people? If you realise that you're micromanaging, you should work to understand why. Do you do it with all your people or just certain ones? Micromanaging suggests a lack of trust, but it can also be brought on by factors within you such as anxiety. If you do it with everyone it's more likely to be coming from within you and you need to address it.

If you micromanage only certain individuals it's probably because you don't trust them to perform. Analyse the reasons. Take the person to one side and let them know you're aware that you're micromanaging them and as it's not your preferred way of working, you want to understand why you're doing it so you can stop. The reasons for a person underperforming can be varied. Do they lack confidence in the role? If so, micromanaging them will make it worse. If you manage them differently you can help to build their confidence if all the other success factors are present. Are they a good fit for the role? An introvert in a customer-facing role may not work out. I know of a company that appointed its ICT manager (who wanted a change but didn't want to leave the company) to the position of Business Development Manager, then wondered why it wasn't working. ICT tends to attract introverts who are happy beavering away quietly in a back room. Introverts are not well suited to BD. So this square peg in a round hole did everything possible to avoid the customer-facing aspects of his role. Eventually they moved him to a more appropriate position.

Is the person underperforming because they have had too little training? If so their ability to perform will be severely handicapped. You can fix this. Do they have personal issues that would be helped by intervention from your Employee Assistance Program?

Finally, it's possible the person is just not suited to the role. You will need to explore other options with them.

Avoid overloading your best people

People's capabilities differ. The people working for you fit somewhere on a spectrum. Some need lots of guidance and support. Others naturally race off after being briefed and do their tasks proficiently and quickly then come back for more. It's tempting to overload your star performers because of their seemingly endless capacity to get things done. I recommend you avoid this. By overloading a high performer, you can turn them into a gibbering wreck, brought to their knees by excessive workload, competing demands on their time and unrealistic expectations that are fed by their own conscientiousness. The high performer becomes a poor performer because they're overloaded. It's easy to do and such people are often their own worst enemies as they're unable to resist taking on more, even when it's too much.

Some years ago I started in a senior role where I had responsibility for several departments including HSE and Quality. I found that the HSE/Quality Manager had been working up to fourteen hours a day trying to cover both roles in this rapidly expanding business. I arranged to split the role; he chose to retain the Quality Manager responsibility, so I appointed another person to take over HSE.

Set limits on authority

Each person needs limits set on their authority and autonomy and for these to be clearly spelled out. These limits serve several functions. They allow you to maintain control over what's happening. They promote clarity about who is responsible for what. They help to ensure that people don't take on responsibilities for which they haven't been trained. They help to prevent over-confident people from going beyond the limits of their competence.

Setting limits is consistent with empowerment. It gives people confidence that they know how far they can go.

How to handle it when things go wrong

Having trained your people, ensured they are supported and spelled out the limits that apply to them, things may still occasionally go wrong. This is when your leadership qualities shine. If you abandon your people to the wolves, they may never trust you again. However, when something goes wrong it's a great opportunity to show your unflinching support and build trust. People feel incredibly vulnerable at times like this. They've messed up and they feel exposed to the full wrath of the higher-ups. You are their protection, the only barrier between them and humiliation and perhaps dismissal. So protect them. Put your job on the line if you must, though hopefully it will never come to that. Ensure justice is done. Not only is this the right thing to do as your people and their work are your responsibility, but you will build a high level of trust and loyalty in your people.

When a team member goes through this sort of ordeal, because it is an ordeal even when you support them, you must then analyse what went wrong and correct the problems.

How do you know if your people feel trusted and empowered?

Empowered people exude confidence. They bounce into your office to discuss an issue, having already thought about a solution and confident you'll listen attentively to them and not ridicule their views. They feel a part of things. It's a great feeling for them and for you.

Exercises

→ Conduct a quick check. Are your people empowered? How did you conclude this?

→ Do you feel empowered?

→ How would you rate the training your company provides to you and your people?

→ How well do you manage your people's workloads?

→ Describe an occasion when you supported one of your people who had made an error.

Chapter 8

What about people who don't trust you?

If you encounter a person who distrusts you, it may not be because of anything you've done.

We all find ways to protect ourselves. If we have experienced hurt such as betrayal of trust, we learn to protect ourselves by not trusting so much or perhaps not at all, in the future.

Each time we meet a situation where trust is required and when we can see the consequences if we trust and are then betrayed, we may shrink back from trusting. We see it as the safer option.

My premise is that human beings naturally want to trust but their ability to trust can be impaired over time due to betrayals big and small. This can be overcome. If you show yourself to be trustworthy without exception, most people will gradually come to trust you. This transition back to trusting is more profound for people who have been badly betrayed. You may earn their undying loyalty by showing them it's safe to trust.

People who are sceptical and untrusting are a challenge to manage. They can be particularly frustrating when you as the leader know the importance of trust, pride yourself on your trustworthiness but are still treated as untrustworthy. If you're in that position, take the sceptic to one side and talk to them about the importance you place on trust. Tell them that you will do everything possible to win and keep their trust. Invite them to bring to you anything they consider a breach of trust on your part and that you will answer their concern. Doing this requires humility (I discuss the importance of this elsewhere) and an acceptance that although you are higher in rank than your people, you believe each of them is your equal in people terms.

In discussions with the person they may reveal the circumstances that have led to them being unable to trust. Trust is a deep issue for most people. If you consider the person would benefit, refer them to the Employee Assistance Program. Persist and in time you'll break through.

Exercises

→ Have you encountered a person who didn't trust you?

→ How did you handle it?

→ Were you able to find out and resolve the cause of the mistrust?

→ Do they trust you now?

Chapter 9

Rebuilding trust

The trust I'm referring to here is trust in you as a leader. Rebuilding trust is a challenge but is not impossible.

What rebuilds trust is the same as what builds trust, with the added element that you need to address what caused the trust to be lost. So the first thing to consider is how the trust came to be absent.

If you have recently started in a role and you find it was your predecessor who caused the loss of trust you will need to begin immediately distancing yourself from your predecessor's ethics and behaviour and demonstrating that you're different.

Be aware that those who resent the appointment of someone to a role, perhaps because they believe it should have been theirs, can try to poison the ground for new incumbent. If this is the case, you'll need to work hard to dispel any false impressions that have been spread. You'll also need to challenge the individuals responsible, if you can identify them.

If you are already established in the role it may be that you are responsible for the loss of trust. You'll need to investigate. You could ask the person in the workforce whom you trust the most and know will give you an honest answer. You will need to find out:

▶ What caused the loss of trust?

▶ How long ago did it happen?

▶ How many people were affected? Is it one person, your team or the whole company?

If something you did caused the breach of trust you should start making amends as soon as you can. The longer the time since the breach of trust occurred, the more effort will be needed to repair it. A long interval means that attitudes will have hardened and people will have given up on being able to trust you. You will need to explain to those affected why nothing has been done about it until now and what you propose to do.

If your employer's action caused trust to be lost, you have a harder task. You will need to believe that the breach is an exception and that top management is unlikely to repeat it, otherwise you too will feel insecure and untrusting and it will be difficult for you to reassure people authentically.

If you are newly arrived in a company and you find values and behaviours not conducive to trust you may need to consider whether you have a future there. Better still you should have evaluated these aspects of a potential employer before you joined!

Exercises

→ Think of a situation you came into where trust in the leadership was lacking.

→ What actions did you take?

→ How did you rebuild trust?

Chapter 10

The power of resentment

Resentment can be defined as "ill feeling caused by a sense of having been badly treated".

Human beings are not perfect. At times we say and do things that give offence and cause resentment.

People may lose trust in you if your actions cause them to feel resentment toward you and you do nothing about it.

The genie of resentment is powerful and once out of the bottle it can be difficult to put back in. Your best approach is never to let it out.

The effects of resentment

People who feel resentment normally want and need to express it. The need may stem from a sense that an injustice has been perpetrated and needs to be corrected, or it may just come from a hunger to get even. People will manifest their resentment across a spectrum ranging from taking no action and just doing a "slow burn" which may be evident only to those close to them, to displaying passive-aggressive behaviour, to being uncooperative when they have no apparent reason to be, to being openly vengeful whenever an opportunity presents itself.

Resentment is corrosive to the person who harbours it and can be long-lived. A resentment created today and not resolved may fester in a person for years and only surface when that person sees the behaviour repeated or sees a chance to get even. By this time the person who caused the resentment will have no recollection of the original incident if they were ever aware of it and may be totally nonplussed at the other person's behaviour that appears to have come out of nowhere.

Unless resolved, resentment never fully goes away because each time the aggrieved person sees the one who created it the resentment is refreshed. You can see the merit of breaking this cycle!

If you have created resentment in someone and you do nothing to remedy it, you are relying on the other person to deal with it. They may not do this very well or they may not do it at all. They probably won't tell you what you've done, especially if you are senior to them in the company. If you are not aware of resentment and how it's created you may not realise you have created resentment. You may observe a negative change in a person's attitude or behaviour toward you or to matters affecting you and be unable to understand why.

People may deflect resentment onto you. They may want to resent the prime leader (who may deserve it) but they can't show resentment to that person so if you're next in line they'll resent you instead!

How is resentment created?

Resentment can be created in many ways, including:

▶ Mistreating or behaving badly toward a person, especially belittling them in front of others.

▶ Behaving as if your rank entitles you to treat others however you like.

▶ Not acknowledging when you have made a mistake that adversely affects a person.

▶ Not making amends to someone you have wronged.

▶ Not explaining the reasons for making a decision that adversely affects a person. For reasons of business confidentiality such explanations cannot always be given but in most cases they can.

People in leadership roles sometimes believe that their position gives them the right to act and behave as they like toward subordinates. If you take this view you're likely to generate a lot of resentment.

How can you identify someone who resents you?

It depends on the depth of the resentment and how it manifests. Usually it is fairly obvious, though some people are better than others at hiding it. Here are some pointers.

▶ Take a clue from facial expressions including micro expressions, and body language. If merely approaching a person causes them to frown or if their body language goes into negative overdrive when you walk up, that may indicate a problem.

▶ Take a reading of the energy a person is projecting toward you. I cannot be specific about how to do this, but you can cultivate the ability. People radiate their thoughts and feelings toward you; if their feelings are strongly negative or positive, you're likely to be able to detect them without a word having to be spoken. I had the experience of meeting for the first time a man who was to become a manager in the company in which I was working as a manager. I happened to be standing in the car park talking with another employee when the new manager walked up. As I looked toward him, I could feel and almost see a wave of negative energy — like the bow wave of a ship — directed at me and preceding him across the car park. Despite my best efforts I never did get on with that individual.

▶ Monitor the person's behaviour toward you. If they display negative responses for no apparent reason this may point to resentment.

Is it resentment or is it dislike because of jealousy?

The reason certain people hold resentment toward you may have nothing to do with any action of yours. Sometimes you don't actually need to do anything to be resented. People can be resented because they join a company, perform well, impress the chief executive and in doing so, displace people who had previously been close to that person. The new person's motivation might be entirely pure but the change in dynamics is enough to seed resentment among those who feel displaced. You may be a high performer who puts your peers in the shade. This may cause you to be treated better than them, for example receiving a bigger share of rewards. Perhaps you'll be promoted over others who've been there longer. Again, you've done nothing wrong but resentment may follow. I've experienced resentment from this cause on occasions.

Your line manager or the chief executive (depending on your reporting relationship) is responsible for balancing the allocation of benefits among the staff so that high performers are appropriately rewarded but not to the exclusion of all others. A failure to manage this can contribute to resentments developing.

However, people are reluctant to show resentment toward a senior person even if they hold them partly responsible, as they risk damaging their relationship with that person. So all their resentment may be directed at you. I believe these situations are often driven by fear, by people taking a benign situation and projecting it into a catastrophe. They fear that their diminished relationship with the chief may lead to discredit, reduced chance of promotion and their eventual exit from the company. This is unlikely; after all they are still valued, it's just that the new person is valued too. There is a chapter on fear in this book because if fear is allowed to thrive, it can power so many other negative effects.

The aggrieved people in this situation become super-sensitised to your behaviour. You can probably never be careful enough to avoid inflaming these people's resentment.

I experienced resentment from a foreman who worked for me. In hindsight I believe this resentment was almost certainly due to the above cause. This person had been in the company from its founding, was from the same foreign country as the MD, and had worked closely with him in the business all along. The foreman was never the number two except perhaps in his own mind, but he and the MD certainly had a strong bond. Then I came along as a new senior manager and instrumental to the company's progress. I think this foreman never quite forgave me for being there. At that time my emotional intelligence was not the highly tuned instrument it is now, so I dealt with his numerous provocations reactively. This gentleman was the one who tried to have me run off the site, as I related previously, such was the depth of his feeling.

People like this are difficult to manage. I would probably do a better job of it now, but I don't know that I could ever have brought him around. We can't save everyone.

How to avoid creating resentment in others

"An ounce of prevention is worth a pound of cure." Being aware of what resentment is and how it is generated helps you to avoid creating it.

The challenge here is that we are much more attuned to the hurts and injustices we suffer than to those we inflict on others. So walk in others' shoes and treat them only in ways that would be acceptable to you. This may sound clichéd but I am merely one of the most recent of many generations that have found it to be true. It is simply the Golden Rule — "Do unto others as you would have them do unto you."

How to resolve resentment from others

When you have identified someone who appears to hold resentment toward you, you need to act quickly lest the relationship become irretrievably toxic. Take the person aside in confidence and talk to them. You may choose to do this away from the workplace. If the person is willing to discuss their concerns, you can work through them and if appropriate consider making amends.

You may be surprised by what the person tells you. It may not have crossed your mind that they could have been upset by a particular event. Perception is reality; it's their perception that matters to them.

You may need to do some soul searching. It's best not to respond immediately but to go away and think about it so you fully understand and empathise with the person's concern. This also gives your ego time to get out of the way. Your immediate response might be to feel affronted, so you need to give yourself time to filter and absorb what you've been told. That said, I recommend you set a time to resume the conversation so the other party knows you are committed to a resolution.

You may conclude that making amends is not necessary. Inform the other person and give them the reasons.

Resentment is a complex response. When resentment is triggered it may be due to a number of factors. Not all resentments can be overcome. But at least you have laid a foundation for avoiding future resentments and you've made clear that you aim to avoid generating them where possible. That's a good start.

How to deal with your own resentment toward others

Resentment is a two-way street. You may be subject to the actions or behaviour of another person that creates resentment in you.

First, don't let it fester and grow by doing nothing about it. You are no different to other people and if you allow resentment to linger within you, it will poison your relations with that person and potentially with others. It's not in your interests to let your resentment become entrenched. By doing nothing you are in effect assuming that the other person intended to cause a hurt. Quite possibly they did not.

Tell the person, irrespective of who they are or what they've done to create the resentment. You'll feel better right away because you've expressed the concern. This will help you to dissipate it. Secondly you've given the other person an opportunity to understand what they've done. They may not be aware. Not everyone understands resentment. They may appreciate it as a learning opportunity and as a chance to make amends. Quite possibly they did not intend to cause hurt. If so they'll appreciate the chance to put it right. This may forge a better bond between you.

You have demonstrated your honest and transparent approach. You've also set a boundary by making clear your expectation that in future the person should not act toward you in that manner.

Finally, you've given yourself a chance to check the person's motives toward you. If on being told of your concern they do not take the opportunity to address it positively, you can probe further to understand why. Perhaps they hold resentment against you for reasons that you know nothing about. If so you can draw them out and address their concerns. At some point it may become apparent to you that the other person is not interested in putting things right between you. If so at least you've done what you can.

It will not benefit your physical or mental health to hold resentment toward a person. One option if you feel aggrieved and amends are not forthcoming is to forgive the person. There are techniques available to help with this. Check the internet under "forgiveness counselling".

CASE STUDY IN RESENTMENT #1 — MY WIFE'S EXPERIENCE

My wife of thirty-plus years is the most caring and considerate person I have ever known. She also has a strong sense of justice.

Many years ago she worked for a company with a brutal and aggressive culture. Her supervisor's manager exemplified this very well. On one occasion he strode into a room full of employees and pointing to each in turn, boasted he could fire that person if he wanted. Needless to say, he was universally despised and feared.

He made a habit of abusing subordinates in front of other employees. One day in front of the work group he verbally abused my wife's supervisor who had limited facility with English.

His abuse extended outside work hours. He would go to the local hotel where his employees drank and continue the abuse there.

My wife and the work group determined to rid the company of this manager. A deputation of employees who had witnessed the abuses went to the head office and filed a detailed report. After an investigation the manager was fired.

In this instance a resentment created over a long period had its just reward.

CASE STUDY IN RESENTMENT #2 — BILLY

A violent verbal disagreement occurred at one of our remote depots between our managing director who was visiting and a crane operator at the depot, Billy. The outcome of this disagreement was that Billy felt bullied and intimidated and left the encounter severely shaken. He stated that he was going straight to his doctor to get put off on stress leave. The managing director was annoyed at Billy's response and the possibility of a stress claim. He felt justified in his anger because Billy had been increasingly uncooperative of recent times.

As the person responsible for human resources and industrial relations, this matter fell in my area. As soon as I heard about the incident, I contacted Billy to assure him that I would thoroughly and impartially investigate.

For a start I enquired at the depot about Billy's work reputation. Apart from an unexplained deterioration over recent months it was very good. A number of our best clients always asked for Billy to be allocated to their sites.

Something didn't add up. So I decided to talk to Billy. The facts came out. Some eighteen months earlier the company had unilaterally increased the rent on his company house by $50.00/week without giving him the required period of notice. So every week he would see this unauthorised extra deduction on his pay slip. It was like being slapped in the face once a week. There was also a long-running unresolved dispute about payment for energy costs in Billy's house.

These issues were running sores that became re-infected each week and never had a chance to heal. Due to the regular reinforcement of Billy's anger he was increasingly on a short fuse at work. This explained his growing lack of cooperation.

Eventually the resentment boiled over and triggered the argument with the MD.

I took action with the MD. I arranged for the company to refund the overcharge for rent, some thousands of dollars, and reach an amicable agreement with Billy on the energy costs. The change in Billy was immediate and striking. A long-standing burden had been lifted and this allowed his true self to shine through. His attitude improved dramatically. I met with him not long after and the change in his appearance was dramatic — the stress had melted from his face and his body. Also he no longer felt the need to pursue the stress claim.

But the damage was done. Billy resigned not long after as he could not altogether overcome his resentment over the matter. However, he left on good terms with no recriminations on either side.

Billy was a senior and influential employee at the depot. I can only speculate on how much damage he did to morale and attitudes within the workforce over a long period and how many customers he poisoned about the company by complaining and spreading negativity.

The lessons from this are:

- ▶ Do what you reasonably can to avoid creating disputes with employees.

- ▶ Identify and resolve disputes as soon as possible after you become aware of them. If you don't, they will fester and morph into bigger issues which may impact the broader workforce and your customers.

- ▶ Adopt a caring and empathetic approach. Put yourself in the employees' shoes.

▶ Acknowledge your or the company's mistakes, if any, and make amends.

That said, I do not advocate a softly-softly approach with troublesome employees. However, I do advocate a zero-tolerance approach: if you see an employee or colleague showing signs of being troubled, don't ignore it — approach the person and find out what's wrong. That's the caring way. Had the depot manager done that with Billy, the truth of what was troubling him would have come out much sooner and could have been addressed before so much damage was done.

The following conditions needed to be met to allow the problem with Billy to be avoided:

▶ The depot manager needed to be better connected with his people and to be interacting regularly with them, not just about work matters, to give him opportunities to pick up on how they were doing.

▶ When the depot manager found that all was not well with Billy, he needed to be willing and able to talk to Billy about it and draw out the cause of Billy's concerns.

▶ Billy needed to trust the depot manager to deal appropriately with his concerns.

The depot manager should have been picking up vibes about Billy from several sources including his foreman, co-workers and customers. He should not have needed to be solely reliant on information coming from Billy. Unfortunately, none of this happened and there was nothing to prevent the Billy saga playing out as it did.

As mentioned elsewhere, troubled employees can be their own worst enemies by alienating people around them with their attitude and behaviour. I suspect that Billy was doing this. Quite possibly the depot manager who applied the rent increase would have been the focus of Billy's antagonism. The proper running of the depot required employees to be flexible in meeting customer requirements. If Billy was being obstructive, he could have become a nuisance to the manager and to his co-workers. If Billy caused problems for the depot manager, the manager would have been less inclined to help him and if Billy's obstructiveness placed stress on his co-workers they too would have been less likely to want to help him. This is a further reason for acting quickly with troubled employees, so this cycle does not have a chance to develop and become entrenched.

Exercises

→ Have you known people who felt resentment toward you?

→ How did you identify this?

→ How long passed from the time the resentment was created until you addressed it?

→ Which of your behaviours have you changed to avoid creating resentment?

→ How good are you at taking the pulse of your people each day so you can pick up any changes in them that require your intervention?

Chapter 11

Fear, and how to avoid leading with it

In recent years I have learned a lot about the power of fear, in some cases through seeing fear used as a tool for control or motivation in the workplace.

Wikipedia has this to say about fear: "Fear is an emotion induced by a threat perceived by living entities, which causes a change in brain and organ function and ultimately a change in behaviour, such as running away, hiding or freezing, when faced with traumatic events. Fear may occur in response to a specific stimulus happening in the present, or to a future situation, which is perceived as a risk to health or life, status, power, security, or in the case of humans, wealth or anything held valuable."

Wikipedia adds the following in regard to anxiety: "Fear should be distinguished from, but is closely related to, the emotion (of) anxiety, which occurs as the result of threats which are perceived to be uncontrollable or unavoidable."

It is said that anger is fear turned outward and depression is fear turned inward. If I encounter an angry person, I look for the fear that is driving the anger. Often I find it and then I can address it but only when the person has calmed down!

Equally if I encounter a depressed person, I look for the fear that is driving the depression. The causes of anger and depression are complex, but knowing their possible connection with fear is a good start to understanding them.

Some people choose to rule by fear. I'm not referring to history's tyrants but to managers and supervisors. You may have encountered some of them. Hopefully you are not one yourself.

Fear works as a motivator in the short term. People can be induced to do things if fear is put into them. It's like the slave driver on the Roman galley cracking the whip over the rowers' backs. But as a motivator, fear destroys trust and negates any sense of care.

A company in Australia for which I was the HSE manager was contracted to a very large global corporation. Every weekday morning at nine am sharp there was a teleconference at the worksite between our site management team and a rather gruff senior person in the client corporation's US headquarters. The purpose of this call was to discuss operational matters including any safety incidents from the last twenty-four hours, the status of investigations of prior incidents and what actions were being taken. My manager normally attended these teleconferences but a couple of times I went along with him.

There was a palpable sense of fear in that room such as I have rarely experienced. Everyone was choosing their words with great care and you could see from facial expressions and body language how stressed, threatened and fearful everyone felt. People in the company had warned me about this but it still came as a shock.

The fear extended to the way people dealt with safety incidents day-to-day. Even a minor incident would trigger a paranoid reaction with everyone running around obsessing about how best to present it at the following morning's conference. For example, one day the bottom beam of a low-loader trailer on our site scraped a high spot on the bitumen causing a small gouge in the bitumen. I recall the site manager being in a state of panic and near-apoplexy as he sought ways to manage the reaction at the next day's conference.

This fear produced tunnel vision that focused people on the reaction that incidents were likely to generate up the line, rather than on prevention. I'm convinced this fear was counterproductive. My approach was to ignore the fear and keep my focus and my team's focus on how to encourage better safety outcomes.

My experience is that rule by fear has more scope to become widespread in larger, more hierarchical companies with more management layers.

People who seek to rule by fear can normally be picked out. Many of them are bullies and cowards. They start by bullying the most vulnerable employees such as young junior females. You may see this and there will be times when you'll need to intervene to deal with such behaviour.

Fear can also be engendered when people feel insecure in their positions, especially when their insecurity is due to a deep-seated belief that they're not worthy of their roles. They can respond to this fear that is their little secret by becoming more arrogant and assertive.

You never need to rule by fear and it is not in your interests to do so.

So what can you personally do? As a leader you can resolve not to rule by fear, not to let others rule by fear, to call out anyone you see trying to rule by fear and to be a role model for creating a fear-free workplace for your team. Your people will appreciate your care and their trust in you will grow. They will talk to others about it. Stories of your leadership will spread. Managers in other sections who still rule by fear will become isolated as they also tend to do when they cannot be trusted. This effect which I have described elsewhere will begin to surface once their own people have seen a better way.

Exercises

→ Have you ever worked for someone who ruled by fear? How did this affect you and others in the team?

→ Have you ever seen safety leadership distorted by fear as in the story I related above?

→ Have you observed other managers become isolated or ostracised by their own teams because they ruled by fear?

Chapter 12

Own your mistakes and make amends

Problems that can stem from strong self-belief

As a leader you need strong self-belief. However, if your self-belief is so strong that you lose perspective it may damage your ability to be trusted. If you combine strong self-belief with an inflated view of your authority derived from your exalted position, you may believe that whatever you do is acceptable. You may think that you can do no wrong, that you cannot be wrong.

There is a link to perfectionism. For example, if when you were a child your parents appreciated you for what you achieved rather than loved you for who you were, as an adult you may have a need to be perfect. In a sense your mind cannot conceive of anything less than your own perfection — which translates to always being right — because to do so carries the risk still lurking in the back of your mind from childhood of not gaining approval or worse still of being rejected.

The problem is that things in life are rarely perfect. Being human, we all make mistakes. What matters when it comes to being trusted is how you handle your mistakes. If you make mistakes or misjudgements that adversely affect others and don't do anything to put them right, you will be generating vast amounts of resentment.

Resentments can be overcome by making amends. Making amends may be the most powerful thing you learn to do to build or rebuild trust. Prior to making amends you need to own your mistakes.

Owning your mistakes

So what is a mistake? Think of it as an action, intentional or unintentional, that had an unintended adverse outcome. It may be an error of judgment where after weighing up all the options, you took action that proved to be incorrect or inappropriate. Perhaps you acted before you had all the information. Perhaps a situation "pressed your buttons" and you overreacted.

In some environments it is just not done to admit mistakes. These environments are often full of fear. You may fear that you will be exposed as imperfect or incompetent and that retribution will follow in the form of public shame or some type of punishment such as denial of promotion or in an extreme, dismissal.

However, as discussed elsewhere there is great power in the truth. The best thing about the truth is that when everything else is stripped away, the truth is all that's left. For example, when we investigate accidents it is truth we seek in the form of the root causes. If we isolate the root causes and put appropriate controls in place, the same type of accident is much less likely to happen again. We avoid outcomes potentially much worse than what happened the first time.

We can try to deny responsibility for our own mistakes

or shift blame to others for them. But people sniff this out because we all have built-in, finely tuned BS detectors. We also have our own ways of finding out what really happened; you talked to someone who was there and who saw it or was at a meeting where evidence about it came out. There are no secrets. The person who tried to cover it up will be found out and trust in that person will evaporate.

You can probably recall people like I've described who never take responsibility for their mistakes. They are universally despised and deeply mistrusted. No one wants to work with or for them. I can only imagine that life for such people is a misery.

Owning your mistakes is a two-part process.

The first is to make a commitment to yourself to acknowledge and own your mistakes and do it each time you make a mistake. Hopefully your mistakes are not too frequent — if they are, that should give you cause to ask why, as those above you will no doubt be doing!

The second, once you're doing the first, is to put yourself in the shoes of people who have been affected by your mistake and feel how it has made them feel. This takes practice but you can learn to do it. Of course, you're not alone in the task and you don't need to speculate about how others are feeling — you just have to ask them. This will bring an immediate benefit and put you on the road to rebuilding your relationship with them.

By asking how your action has made someone feel, you are showing care and concern. When you show care, you build trust. Asking the question shows that you want to know the answer; once you have the answer you can move to put things right.

Feeling is a heart function, not a head function, so it's

different to processes that you might bolt on to existing skills. Fortunately, we all have hearts and we all feel. Technical specialists are trained to be good at processes — for example, designing computers or analysing geological samples. But as technical people we're not so good at bringing our feelings to work. Our empathetic side can become subordinated to the needs of the technical side. This effect is magnified when we're in a company full of technical specialists. Technical people need to work harder to bring the feeling side out.

So why not decide to own your mistakes from now on? You stand to gain a lot.

Firstly, in an environment filled with fear where 'fessing up is not the norm, you'll stand out in a positive way. People will come to see that owning their mistakes does not have to lead to negative consequences; in fact, by your example you will begin to change the culture and drive fear away.

Secondly, by owning your mistakes you'll facilitate the process of finding out what went wrong. This is crucial and not just for incident investigations. If you want your company's performance to improve you must discover the real causes of what goes wrong so they can be remedied. When you don't own your mistakes, you signal that you're closed off to finding the truth. Unwanted outcomes usually have a number of causes. You need to create an environment in which people feel safe to identify these causes. If you own your actions that contributed to a negative event and show that you don't fear doing so, people are far more likely to come forward with information that will help reveal the full story.

Thirdly you'll feel better. Concealing the truth of your own responsibility or trying to place blame on others comes at a personal cost. There is a small voice inside telling you what you're doing is wrong. Every time you ignore it, you're being untrue to yourself and you whittle away some of your being.

Fourthly and most importantly, you'll build trust. People know that people make mistakes. No one is immune from making mistakes and if you pretend to be, you'll lose credibility and trust. However, if those around you know that you always acknowledge and own your mistakes they'll have much more trust in you. Your example will encourage them to act the same way.

So the first step is to practise taking responsibility for your mistakes. At first it will feel foreign if you're not used to it. In time it will get easier. Be prepared for other people to start seeing you in a different light. Their perceptions will take time to change; they need to see consistency in your new behaviour so they come to believe that you will maintain it and they can come to trust you.

Now that you're learning to own your mistakes you will see the world differently and the world will see you differently. You'll feel less threatened by the risk of unpleasant facts coming out as they have in the past despite your furtive but furious efforts to suppress them. You'll find that you can be yourself, a persona that perhaps you have not inhabited for a long time. A lot of stress will melt away. It takes energy and effort to hold up a façade. You'll no longer need to do that. You'll have more usable energy because you're not using part of your energy to maintain a false front.

By your actions you'll be showing people a different and better way to live. No one who experiences it will want to go back. You may find fewer people around you who still do it the old way because many have seen the light and changed. Any who have not will be increasingly isolated. In such ways is the culture of a company changed. I have seen this in action and it's wonderful. Those who won't change, even senior people, start to lose their moral authority. The focus of their subordinates moves toward those who are more enlightened. This applies pressure to the ones still stuck in the old ways.

Part of the change will be that you'll see more clearly the effect your actions have on people. Previously you were closed off to that; you had to be because to acknowledge it you would have had to admit that your whole approach was wrong. You may be shocked by what comes out, particularly when you start making amends to those people.

Returning now to making amends, seeing and feeling the effects your actions have on people is what gives energy to making amends. So what is making amends and how do you start?

What does "making amends" mean?

There are few deeds more powerful in relationship building and repair than making amends.

The Encarta Dictionary defines amends as "something done or given as compensation for a wrong". So in making amends we are doing or giving something as compensation for a wrong.

That something is usually an apology, at least as a start. If it's to be genuine, an apology should not be offered lightly, as it carries a burden of responsibility. If it's not genuine there's no point; it's just hollow meaningless words. An insincere apology will destroy trust, not build it. The responsibility that comes with an apology is to feel remorse for the effects of what you've done and to make yourself a commitment not to repeat the behaviour or action. So it's something to take seriously.

Whether more than an apology is called for depends on

the circumstances. If a person has suffered loss you should look for ways to make restitution. Consider the nature of the loss. For example if you have belittled a person in front of their peers, they have suffered humiliation and compensation would come in the form of you apologising to the person in the presence of those same people. If a person has suffered financial loss you should consider ways to help them recoup the loss as in the situation with Billy where I arranged for the company to make restitution by refunding an overcharge of rent on his company house.

Learning how to make amends

Now you're making progress; you're learning to acknowledge your mistakes and you're noticing that people appreciate it and respond positively. You're seeing and feeling the effect your actions have on others. You have learned to question others to find what the effect of your actions has been. So now you can begin to make amends.

Start with a sincere apology, given to the person one-on-one.

Some people will have been so badly affected by your actions, particularly if trust has been compromised, that at first they'll be resistant to receiving an apology. They may not even want to engage with you. The problem for them is that if they haven't dealt fully with the original hurt, receiving an apology can bring it all back and cause them to relive the pain. Before apologising you may need to assure them that you're genuine in your intent. This will certainly be the case if you're not known as a person who makes amends. If you offer to apologise and the other person reacts emotionally you will have gained further insight into the effects of your actions.

If the action for which you have apologised was committed in front of others, after you apologise one-on-one you should make the apology in front of those present when the original act was committed. At first this can be even harder than making the initial apology and may appear to involve loss of face on your part. But how often has someone apologised only to you for something they did in the presence of others? How did you feel? What value did the apology have? How did this shape your perception of that person? Consider all this when deciding how to make your apology.

People who are not accustomed to making amends may find it difficult and uncomfortable at first. But when you do it, you'll grasp the tremendous payback it offers and each time you do it you'll build muscle strength.

In making amends a personal approach works best irrespective of how many people are involved. If you're making amends to a work group, address them all. Let them see you face-to-face, know that your concern is genuine and that you have nothing to hide.

Sweep your side of the street

In most situations of conflict, both parties have contributed to some degree. So how do you proceed if you want to apologise for your part, but the other person shows no sign of doing the same?

What would I do? I would apologise anyway. This approach was paraphrased by a colleague as 'sweeping your side of the street'. It means doing the right thing, as you see it, irrespective of what the other person does.

We cannot force another person to apologise. Or maybe we

can by pulling rank, but an apology extracted this way would be of little value to them or to you. There are exceptions such as mediated settlements but in general a person must want to apologise. Your action in apologising first will make it easier for them to apologise.

Many people are not good at apologising. Some have been brought up to believe that it is a sign of weakness. A person may have resentment against you for something entirely unrelated and this makes them reluctant to apologise. They may not be as evolved as you. They may have a lower emotional intelligence than you. They may not have experienced making a heart-felt apology and seeing the benefits that flow for them and for the recipient. They may not have analysed the situation as you have and seen what is needed. Whatever the reason there is no need to condemn a person who is reluctant to apologise. You can lead the way by doing it yourself. In my experience they'll usually follow.

Hopefully a genuine apology from you brings a reciprocal apology. Then the parties can discuss ways to fix the problem and avoid a recurrence, freed from the resentment of unacknowledged responsibility. But even if you are the only one who has apologised you have at least removed any impediment to progress from your side.

Your action in apologising has several effects:

▶ It removes a barrier to the other party apologising.

▶ It sets an example to the other person.

▶ It lets them see the benefits of apologising, for example how it clears the air and reduces tension.

- ▶ It lets them see that apologising is not as difficult as they may have thought.

- ▶ It shows others that you're not above making amends for your actions. This may well inspire them to do likewise and this will positively influence the culture of the company.

The timing of an apology

An apology should be offered and made as soon as possible after the event or as soon as you realise what you've done, but only after you've calmed down and given the other party time to cool off. An apology offered when both parties are still caught up in the moment is likely to be counterproductive.

Grudging or insincere apologies

Before apologising you need to have come to a full acceptance of the need to apologise. A grudging or insincere apology is of little value. You must be genuine.

Conditional apologies

An apology that comes with conditions is close to useless. It may be worse than useless because instead of restoring trust it can further erode it. So only make your apologies with a good heart, when you can do so genuinely and unconditionally.

How often do I personally make amends?

I've devoted a lot of space to detailing the importance of making amends. It must sound like a vast amount of apologising is going to be needed. It shouldn't be. When you decide to start making amends, you'll probably have a few amends to make at first. As you come to understand what causes hurt and resentment, you'll get better at not causing it and the need for you to make amends will reduce.

Personally I make amends once or twice a month. Most instances are minor; largely I've learned not to do things that will call for an apology later.

So you've apologised — what now?

Making an apology reflects an understanding of the effect of what you did and implies a feeling of remorse linked to an intention not to repeat the behaviour. What's the point of apologising if you just repeat the behaviour? For people to see an apology as genuine it needs to be followed up by a change in behaviour that is consistent with the apology. For the person making the apology this sets a standard for future actions. To be seen as trustworthy you need to live up to that standard. You may cause hurt or resentment with other actions but hopefully never again with this one.

Once you have experienced the benefits of making amends you will almost certainly continue to do it as a matter of course. It's especially useful for relationship maintenance. In your daily interactions with your work colleagues and friends you can be unconsciously scanning for resentments and if you find any, you can draw people out about them and move to set things right.

The need for you to make amends should become less frequent as you become more attuned to avoiding the creation of resentments. As well, once people around you understand your approach, they'll be less likely to develop resentment against you because they'll understand you're actively trying to avoid creating resentment and they'll give you the benefit of the doubt.

All the foregoing does not mean that as you relate to people your whole focus should be on looking for resentments you might have caused. It is just one of many aspects of your interactions. My experience is that as you become more adept at avoiding resentments the process quickly blends into your subconscious and only surfaces when you detect that something is amiss.

When you're aware of resentment and its causes, it soon becomes clear which people around you have that same awareness. Those who don't have it stand out like bulls in china shops as they charge around generating ill feeling.

What if you believe you are in the right?

My recommendation to make amends applies only if there is justification for making amends.

If after careful consideration and having explored the situation thoroughly from the other person's perspective you conclude you have done nothing for which you need to apologise, there will be nothing to be gained from you making an apology.

It builds relationships when people know you consider yourself answerable for your actions.

Exercises

→ Do you take responsibility for your mistakes?

→ Is there someone in your work group to whom you need to make amends?

→ Consider how you will make amends to them: where you will do it, whether it will be in the presence of others, what you will say and how you will handle their response.

→ Go ahead and make the apology then review how it went. Did the other person appreciate it? Did they reciprocate? How did you feel?

Chapter 13

The magic of caring

This is your invitation into a world where people are well cared for at work. If you're already there, that's great; you are reaping at least some of the rewards and this chapter will provide additional insights to help you maximise the benefits.

If you do not inhabit a working world where people are well cared for it may be because you or those around you do not yet fully appreciate the benefits. If so this chapter will help you come to a full understanding.

There is boundless potential for improving the care you show your workforce. I invite you to be creative and engage your people in devising new and better ways of caring.

Leading your people with care has many wonderful benefits. One is that you will give your people every reason to stay and no reason to leave.

If a company intends to become one that cares for its people, the driving force in words and deeds must come from the top. If the person at the head of the company has an uncaring attitude it is much more difficult for those lower in the chain to show care. They will believe that a lack of care is acceptable because the chief is modelling that behaviour. They know that they will not be criticised or held accountable if they don't show care. Some will show care anyway because that's the way they're wired; many will not unless it is modelled for them.

I believe that given a choice most of us would prefer to live and work in a caring environment rather than among people who don't care for or about us. That is not to say we're all weaklings who cannot survive and thrive without care. My experience is simply that people do better with care.

Research also supports the notion that caring for your people brings about better safety outcomes. I discuss this in Chapter 14.

When I refer to "caring" I am not talking about caring that a caregiver provides for a disabled or infirm person. There is no suggestion that your people need this type of care. I am referring to your caring attitude toward them and about them, your ability to empathise with them and their needs and to respond appropriately.

My "ah-ha moment" about caring

It took one incident for me to begin to realise the importance of caring.

In 1996 my employer was asked to set up an off-road tyre service and management operation on the world's largest copper mine, 10,000 feet (3,150 metres) above sea level in the Andes of northern Chile. The client specifically asked that I be brought in to run the operation and in late 1996 I moved to Chile.

The workforce was similar to that on the Australian tyre operation described elsewhere. The superintendents who ran the workshop reported to me and worked back-to-back, four days on followed by three days off, overlapping by one day that we used for briefings. The only expatriate in the workforce apart from me was one of the workshop superintendents who came with me from Australia. All my other employees including the other workshop superintendents were Chilean.

The Chilean service people worked on a two-and-one roster: two weeks on shift followed by one week off. Some of these workers lived in central Chile, a fifteen-hour bus ride south of the mine. At the end of their two weeks on site they would catch the overnight bus home, spend a few days there then catch a bus back to site.

In July of 1997 there was a major earthquake in central Chile. Many mud brick homes were destroyed including one belonging to Andrés T, one of our tyre servicemen.

The earthquake was reported on the news but I was not aware that one of our people had been caught up in it until informed by one of my superintendents, Carlos H. I casually enquired as to the cost of repairs to Andrés' house, thinking it would be in the thousands or even the tens of thousands of dollars. Carlos replied that Andrés would only need US$200 for materials then with help from his family and friends he would rebuild his home.

Reaching into my desk drawer I pulled out the company chequebook, wrote out a cheque to Andrés for US$200, signed it and asked Carlos to give it to him.

At the time what I did was no more than a reflex action. At minimal cost I could help Andrés get back on his feet. However, the effect was magical. A few days later Carlos mentioned that Andrés had been telling his workmates what the company had done and had added, 'After this, if they want to get rid of me they'll have to carry me out of here in a box!'

I subsequently reflected on the enormous significance of this for Andrés. Through a simple act that cost me nothing, albeit done with good and pure intention, I had shown great care and compassion for him and helped him rebuild not only his house but also his life and his family's life.

The personal effect on Andrés inevitably flowed through to his work as reflected in what he said to his workmates. Andrés himself had become tightly bonded to the company, a wave of positivity spread through the workforce fed by Andrés' delight and relief at having been given the means to rebuild his life and Andrés no doubt influenced others positively, especially any who were wavering in their views of the company and its benevolent and caring attitude.

All of this could have untold positive consequences in a company. It is a small leap to postulate that following this incident, employees in general became more cooperative, employees who might have been planning to leave the company decided to stay, good prospective employees were attracted to join and employees in general had more trust in the company and its management. All of this no doubt led to a more positive working environment.

Such is the power of caring.

Around this time, I acquired among my Chilean workforce the nickname "Grandma's Heart", a term reserved for people considered thoughtful and compassionate but also a bit of a soft touch. Things were improving!

At the time I cannot claim to have fully understood and applied the lessons of this event but over time this incident has had a profound effect on the way I treat my people. More and more since then I've made it my mission to apply the principles of care wherever I can.

In my management roles in recent years I have actively sought to care for my employees as a priority. I believe that my work has had much better outcomes as a result.

In fact I came to view my relationships with my people through a lens of care. I explain this below.

The power of caring is applicable well beyond the working environment. I believe we should all strive to apply the principles of caring throughout our lives.

So how did this event help my transition to becoming a leader? Simply put, it opened my eyes. Through this incident, one essential element of leadership — caring for my people — was revealed to me. It remains a cornerstone of my approach.

But caring acts in isolation aren't enough. Other elements are required. Had I done a caring act for the people involved in the saga of the pens, it would have meant nothing to them and they would have brushed it aside.

How trust and care are related

Care is a subset of trust. When you are trusted you can show care for people and it will be well received. If you are not trusted, any caring acts you perform are likely to be discounted.

The lens of care

I wear glasses. I need help with my close vision for reading and with distance vision for driving. So in the one pair of glasses I have lenses that seamlessly blend three focal lengths in different parts of the lens: reading at the bottom, long distance at the top and intermediate distance in between.

My uncorrected vision isn't that bad — I'm just about legal to drive without glasses but I struggle to read small print without them. With glasses I see differently and more clearly.

The event in Chile I described earlier helped me realise that there was a different kind of lens, a lens of care, through which I could view life and my relations with people differently and more clearly.

I now try to view every interaction with people through this lens of care. I am constantly on the lookout for ways to care better for the people around me. In some instances nothing changes, but in many cases it does. I make a conscious effort to see situations through the eyes of others and to take their perspective into account before I respond. This took effort over a period of years. I had long-established habit patterns to change.

Helping people as part of caring

As a caring leader you naturally want to help people, especially if you perceive they need help. However you cannot help people unless they acknowledge they need help, that they have done everything possible themselves, that they can do no more and are now powerless over the problem.

The founders of Alcoholics Anonymous (AA) understood this. The principle became enshrined as step one of the AA twelve-step program:

Step 1. We admitted we were powerless over alcohol — that our lives had become unmanageable.

The context here is alcohol addiction, however I believe this is a universal principle when it comes to helping people. Have you ever tried to help someone whom you believed needed help but who hadn't yet accepted this? What was the outcome? I can guess: they politely declined your offer whilst vehemently denying that they had a problem or that they needed help from you or anyone else. Perhaps they were affronted. Perhaps they resented you. Perhaps they drew back making it harder to offer them help in the future.

I have had great success helping people and getting help for them once they acknowledged they needed help. When people have reached this place, provided they trust you they will be open to whatever you can do for them and anything is possible. Up to that point your offers are likely to be rebuffed.

However, your offer of help even if declined can be enough to give a person hope. If people are in a difficult situation or one in which they feel there is no hope, it's very important for them to see that there is hope. An offer of help gives them that hope.

In 2000 I was very depressed and was contemplating suicide. I had not let on to anyone about my state of mind. Fortunately, I decided to go to a doctor and get help. The doctor was very understanding and mapped out a program, including medication. He also asked me if I wanted to be admitted to a medical facility until I overcame the desire to commit suicide. I said to him: 'No thanks, that won't be necessary. Now I have hope.' Such is the power of hope.

Exercises

→ Have you had an experience that showed you how important it is to show care for your people?

→ Do you consider that you show care for your people? If so, how do you do this?

→ Do you believe your people would agree that you show them care?

→ Have you ever tried to help someone who hadn't yet accepted that they needed help? What was the outcome?

Chapter 14

How to show care

The following are some ways you can show care for your people.

Make a personal care commitment to new-hires

Employees look to the leadership of a company to set the culture and tone for their employment. This process is best begun when an employee is inducted upon starting work.

As a part of inducting new employees and re-inducting existing employees, you would normally go through the company's policies and values statement and give each person a copy. This is an excellent time to embed in people's minds your commitment to caring. You can demonstrate this most effectively by having your company's chief executive:

▶ Open each company induction in person.

▶ Make a very brief welcoming statement.

▶ Look each inductee in the eye, tell them that safety

is personal in this company and is much more than just a set of processes and procedures, important as these are.

- ▶ Make a personal commitment to each person to do their utmost to protect that employee's safety and wellbeing at work.

- ▶ Invite each person to tell them if they perceive any action taken by the company or its officers is at odds with this commitment.

The address needs to be kept short — thirty seconds or less — with no preaching and no exhortations to work hard, just a straightforward message focused on the commitment to care.

If the chief executive cannot be there, a senior manager can deputise. A last option is to show a short video segment of the chief executive making the commitment. This is less effective than having that person or their designate there particularly if the person doesn't come across convincingly on screen.

To many employees, the effect of such a commitment is electrifying. People are accustomed to the notion of care being more of an abstract concept if indeed it's considered at all, rather than a matter that is front and centre and clearly so important to top management that they talk openly about it and make a face-to-face commitment about it.

Some benefits of making such a clear commitment are:

- ▶ Employees see from the outset the importance that the company places on their welfare. I have seen this type of commitment discussed with wonderment among blue-collar employees. I have seen evidence that new employees are so struck by the commitment that they have recommended the company to their friends as a great employer.

- ▶ A standard is set for all and then has to be met. Top management must shape its approach to align with the commitment or risk being seen as hypocritical.

- ▶ The commitment also creates an expectation that employees will work to protect their own safety and wellbeing.

Insulate your people from the excessive demands of higher-ups

A company of which I was a director placed teams of people onto remote sites to carry out electrical commissioning. On one project the commissioning manager although supportive was at times fractious even though our company's work was of a very high standard. We later found out that this commissioning manager had been under fierce and unrelenting pressure from his project director. Despite this he had protected and insulated us from this pressure. This manager certainly passed the test of leadership and character.

Bring values into your company

What are values? Values are qualities of character that define people, companies and products or services at their most basic level. They establish a foundation on which expectations and trust are built, and they generate behaviour.

Values lie at the heart of a company's culture. Taking responsibility for planning their values allows a company to create its corporate culture with confidence. Once defined values are in place, they provide a roadmap for how the company conducts business.

We have seen that as a manager of people you're a leader whether you accept it or not. There is a parallel with company values; your company has a set of values whether you accept it or not.

Company leaders must take responsibility for the values the company, its directors, its employees, its products and its services manifest.

If a company has defined values that have been formally and consultatively developed, are regularly workshopped, are actively lived day-to-day and woven into the company's fabric, then those are the values.

If there are no defined values, the default values kick in. These are the personal values, attitudes and prejudices of top management, reflected in their behaviour and transmitted to everyone in the company. Depending on the character of these senior people, the default values may not be positive. For example, if the chief executive has clawed his or her way to the top by bullying, a default value will be that it's OK to bully, and this behaviour will be replicated down through the ranks creating a company that's very unpleasant to have as your employer.

If your company does not already live by a defined set of values, I strongly recommend you become an advocate for introducing them.

Defined values are typically expressed as a brief set of words or phrases that encapsulate the company's ethics and aspirations and to which all people in the company can relate.

A long-winded value set is likely to miss the point because people will struggle to identify with it. Values need to be positive and specific.

At their best, a company's values are developed consultatively so everyone or at least a majority feels ownership of them because they've been involved in creating them.

However, the consultative approach needs to be guided. In one company in which I worked the values set was a long-winded catchall generated from wide workforce consultation and was unwieldy. It missed the mark because employees could not relate to it.

The pursuit of profit is not a value. In for-profit companies, a profit motive is integral to survival and prosperity and is not optional. Even in not-for-profits, revenue must exceed spending to ensure the organisation's ongoing viability.

Once values are in place, they should be workshopped with all employees so everyone understands their deeper significance, what each value means to them individually and what behaviours reflect the values. You need to repeat the workshops at intervals, partly to ensure you catch new people and partly to reinforce the understanding of and commitment to the values among existing people.

When values are thoroughly embedded, one finds them entering the everyday life of the company and people referring to them in conversations. Someone might say 'I complimented Bob today because his behaviour really showed that he was living our values'. People can also be reminded if they are not living the values.

I have worked in companies that lived by values that were widely published, included in company documentation, workshopped regularly and universally understood. It was a great experience, not least because of the bonding that took place when the values were being discussed. Such workplaces certainly feel special.

Some of my employers didn't have values. When you have worked in a company with strong values it feels hollow when you move to a company that doesn't have them. There is a definite sense that something is missing. Values add a dimension of meaning, a higher purpose, to the simple equation of working for a wage.

I heard of a company that started out with strong values but lost sight of them over time and ceased living by them. That would have been very difficult. I gather it didn't happen overnight. Evidently it could be traced to a significant setback the company experienced in its fortunes. This had a bad effect on some of the top management. Reportedly the decline started with an increasing level of disputation among the directors. Nothing was done to investigate and fix the causes of the bad feeling or to halt the disputes. Behaviour that would never have been tolerated began to be condoned. Some of the more vulnerable employees such as younger females began to be subjected to verbal abuse and bullying. I understand that many of the longer-term employees who had joined because they were attracted by the previous strong values, simply left. Some were heard to say that the place just wasn't the same anymore.

It cannot be said that this company failed when it lost its values. However, the full story has yet to be written. I can say that for people in the company who knew it when it had strong values it was a distressing experience to see the values being eroded. It also destroyed faith and trust in the MD because earlier on he was the primary driver of the values and then he was seen to be the one letting them dissipate.

A company with strongly espoused values creates a

standard by which it is judged internally and externally. You put values out there because you want clients to know what you stand for. My experience is that clients and prospective clients see an extra dimension to companies that have strong values compared to those that don't. I believe in part it's because they see such companies as more like their own company or more like they aspire to be. I also believe there is a perception that if a company has taken the time to develop and embed values it must already have mastery over its core business. This perception helps customers to develop the all-important trust in the company.

Eliminate bullying

Bullying is one of the most corrosive and destructive behaviours that people can face in the workplace. If you eliminate it from your company, you will serve many ends including showing great care for your people.

Wikipedia defines workplace bullying as 'a persistent pattern of mistreatment from others in the workplace that causes either physical or emotional harm. It can include such tactics as verbal, nonverbal, psychological, physical abuse and humiliation.' A bullying act affects more than just the immediate victim. Employees who witness or hear about the incident become very stressed and are left feeling insecure. So a great deal of avoidable stress is eliminated when you stamp bullying out. Employees feel a sense of gratitude knowing that they no longer need to brace themselves in case it happens again.

In one company where I worked, I managed to substantially stamp out bullying. It was a major problem when I joined: I was receiving one report of bullying or harassment every week. I investigated each one and if the complaint was justified, I took action against the perpetrator(s). Usually the first move was a verbal warning that the company would not tolerate the behaviour and if it happened again a written warning would be issued. Offenders could see a path to eventual dismissal if they persisted. This was normally enough to deter them.

Without naming those involved I publicised the outcome of each investigation at a daily pre-start meeting at the location where the incident occurred so people understood that if they bullied it would be reported and they would be investigated.

However, the most successful measure I took was to educate everyone in the company about what bullying is, what its legal consequences are and that everyone has a right to work without being bullied. In the past, people had accepted bullying because they didn't know any different. They just thought it was the way people behaved in the robust culture of this construction company.

As the education program was rolled out the number of bullying complaints initially increased. People who had received the training could now see bullying for what it was, knew they didn't have to tolerate it and felt empowered to report it knowing that action would be taken.

Over twelve months the rate of complaint dropped to zero. That is not to say bullying disappeared entirely, though its most overt manifestations did. The people who had an ingrained tendency to bully continued to do it in less obvious ways, but I know that employees in general were a lot happier and felt much less threatened, stressed and apprehensive.

To me the most interesting aspect of the virtual elimination of bullying was that the remaining handful of individuals, unfortunately all senior managers, who were known bullies and had not altogether changed their ways, were ostracised even by employees in their own departments. Of course, people still took direction from them but used every opportunity to isolate them. This was a significant shift.

Such is the power unleashed by caring.

Help your people achieve their higher purpose

What is a higher purpose? It's a belief that there is more to life than just working to live. It means making the best of oneself. It means striving to find the highest expression of your talents, abilities and character. For many it means reaching into the spiritual realm to find meaning.

People can work just for a wage or salary. In a company that does not have strongly held values or where the one unspoken value is profit, that's usually what they do. However, employees respond positively to their leader's acknowledgement that there is a higher purpose in life and to their support in pursuing it.

American psychologist Abraham Maslow developed the theory of a hierarchy of need. Simply put, this states that as people satisfy certain basic needs such as shelter and food, they move on to wanting and needing to satisfy higher order needs. One such higher order need is that of self-actualisation. Self-actualisation means self-fulfilment, the realisation of one's own full potential. You can see that just turning up to work each day to perform drudgery isn't going to move a person toward self-actualisation.

If as a leader you are aware of human drives such as the need for self-actualisation, you can help your people satisfy them. This involves knowing what makes each of your people tick and what constitutes self-actualisation for them.

To do this provides an extra dimension of meaning to employment. People recognise how special this is and are reluctant to leave such environments.

At times in my mentoring work I have advised mentees that they should consider taking up a different career, more challenging and more likely to lead to self-actualisation than their current one. For some this would have meant leaving the company for which we both worked. I would always prefer an individual to achieve their highest purpose even if it meant them having to pursue it elsewhere.

Lead and manage safety well

The primary aim of leading and managing safety well is to protect your people. There are few better ways to show care and build trust than looking after your people through vigorous and well-applied safety management. I cover this in detail in Chapter 17.

Create and actively promote an Employee Assistance Program (EAP)

An EAP — counselling for employees that is free to them and anonymous if they self-refer — is a powerful tool for:

▶ Helping employees to overcome personal or work issues that are troubling them.

▶ Creating a workforce that is more focused and productive.

▶ Reducing employee distractions at work.

▶ Demonstrating care for employees.

Counselling refers to a professionally trained person, a counsellor or psychologist, working with an individual to help them resolve troubling issues and providing tools and techniques to help the individual respond more constructively in the future.

Many of the issues counsellors work with involve an individual's relationships. Data for companies where I have introduced and run EAPs suggests that two-thirds or more of issues brought to counselling are personal rather than work-related and that many have the potential to distract employees and compromise their ability to work safely and productively.

A likely consequence of providing and actively promoting an EAP is that employees feel more bonded to the company, so employee retention improves.

In larger companies EAPs are very common however in my experience many EAPs are poorly promoted so they end up under-utilised.

The EAP provider — internal or external?

Let us assume that your company does not currently have an EAP and that you plan to introduce one. You'll need to consider whether the EAP service should be provided by a department within the company or by an external provider. To date I have used only external providers for the following reasons:

▶ Trust is all-important. If employees are to be comfortable to use the service they need to trust that no information will flow back from the counsellor to the company. Counsellors are ethically bound not to disclose to the employer information revealed through counselling. However, perception is reality. If employees perceive a risk of information from counselling being passed to their employer, they may be reluctant to use the EAP. An external provider being functionally separate from the employer increases the prospect that employees will trust the process.

▶ Given that only 5-10% of employees typically use the services of an EAP, most companies will not have enough EAP traffic to justify an in-house EAP. An external provider can make counselling available when needed and charge only for services delivered.

▶ An in-house provider could not cover the diversity of counsellor expertise and experience that an external provider with its greater number of counsellors can.

▶ When a company has a dispersed network of sites, the internal EAP option becomes even less viable. An external EAP provider is more likely to have counsellors available in major population centres closer to remote sites.

▶ An internal EAP requires professional staff dedicated to it. Because of their specialised skills these people cannot perform other tasks in the company if they're not busy doing EAP work so there may be unproductive time that still costs the company money.

► As a separate department, an EAP would require structure and management, increasing costs.

Initial promotion of the EAP

One of my first questions after joining a company in a senior role was: 'Do we have an EAP?' The answer was 'Yes, we do have an external provider EAP.' Good start. My next question was: 'How do we promote it?' The response was: 'When we launched it six months ago, we sent out an email telling everyone about it. The email mentioned that employees are limited to six sessions.' When I checked utilisation of the EAP it came as no surprise that not a single person had accessed it.

So I embarked on a campaign to promote the EAP. I have found the best way to promote an EAP initially is face to face. At each company site I visited I addressed pre-start meetings and toolbox safety meetings and spoke about the EAP. If you are talking about your company's EAP at employee meetings you need to mention that:

► We all have problems and challenges in our personal and working lives and sometimes we can benefit from outside help in dealing with them.

► An EAP is the way our company makes this service available to you.

► The EAP service is free to you. All you need to do is contact the provider and make an appointment.

▶ What you discuss with the counsellor is totally confidential. The company will never be told.

▶ The service is anonymous if you self-refer. You make the appointment yourself and you do not need to inform the company that you are attending counselling. A visit to an EAP counsellor is normally done in work time using personal leave so an application for personal leave would need to be made but without giving the reason.

▶ There are many benefits to seeking counselling through an EAP. Here are some:

→ Counsellors are independent. They are not a partner or family member, not a friend or workmate and not your supervisor or manager. So their advice is not biased by their knowledge of you or by any emotional attachment.

→ Counsellors are professionally trained. Many have degrees in psychology in addition to their counsellor training. They will not solve your problems — only you can do that — but they will provide you tools to enable you to do it yourself. By using these tools you will understand your role in past situations and respond differently in future.

→ During counselling sessions, the counsellors give you their undivided attention. For the duration of each session you are their sole concern and they are not distracted by people coming into the office asking questions or by having to take phone calls. So you are able to have a very focused conversation.

Often after I have given EAP introductory briefings, managers report to me that people from their team approached them to raise personal issues and to seek advice as to whether they should access the EAP. The managers invariably encouraged these employees to set up initial EAP sessions.

The EAP should also be introduced at the initial company induction using the format above so each new employee knows about it from the first day of their employment.

The EAP provider normally has explanatory leaflets available and these should be handed out to new employees as part of their induction pack and to existing employees during re-inductions and information sessions.

Ongoing promotion of the EAP

The above process gets the EAP off to a good start. It is then necessary to keep it front and centre with people at least until momentum builds to a point where EAP use becomes commonplace and self-sustaining. Managers can do this by periodically addressing people at pre-start meetings or toolbox meetings to remind them about the availability of the EAP service.

In time, usually fairly quickly, the EAP becomes an accepted part of the company's suite of offerings. Promotion of the EAP then enters a new phase where managers, supervisors or employees who have used and benefited from the EAP become unofficial ambassadors for it. It moves out of the realm of something that is just sponsored by management, and therefore potentially suspect in the eyes of some, and enters the fabric of the company. See the reference to the Operations Superintendent in case study two below. It becomes common for employees to refer other employees — usually their friends — to the EAP when they perceive a need.

Ways you can use an EAP

You can use an EAP in the following ways:

- ▶ Direct self-referral. The individual contacts the EAP provider and makes a booking.

- ▶ A recommendation to access the EAP from a manager or workmate to whom an employee brings concerns. The employee may contact the EAP or ask his supervisor to do it.

- ▶ Intervention in cases of trauma such as the suicide of a workmate.

- ▶ Intervention and trauma counselling after a serious work accident.

- ▶ Mandatory referral of individuals to the EAP after detection of alcohol or illicit drugs. Normally in such cases the employee must attend EAP counselling until the counsellor considers they have completed sufficient sessions.

Case studies of EAP success

CASE STUDY #1 — SUICIDE PREVENTED

A casual (i.e., non-permanent) employee was working on a

remote site some 300 kilometres from head office. He lived in a town near the site so rarely visited head office.

One day he came into head office and asked to see me. He started by thanking me for making the EAP available to him as a casual employee and explained that it had saved his life. He said that he had been going through a very tough time in his personal life, that his marriage had broken down leading to separation and that his young children had been badly affected by it. He had spiralled into depression and seeing no way out was planning to take his own life. He eventually confided his state of mind to a workmate who recommended he access the EAP. He did so and had several sessions of counselling. He credits these and the tools and techniques he gained through them to saving his life.

It is sobering to contemplate that this human being is still walking the earth largely because of the intervention of an EAP.

CASE STUDY #2 — DEALING WITH GRIEF

The Managing Director told me he had been receiving hate mail delivered anonymously via the company website feedback page. He was deeply troubled by this and asked me to investigate.

On checking I found that a recent ex-employee from one of our depots had committed suicide. Although his suicide was not related to his employment there were many people at the depot who had been friends with the former employee and who were grieving over his loss.

I called a meeting with employees who were friends of the deceased. I downloaded a one-page summary of the Kübler-Ross *Five stages of grief* from the internet and printed copies. On entering the room where these ten folk were gathered, it was immediately clear that they were suffering badly. After a brief introduction I handed out the pages I had printed and explained the five stages of grief. Then I talked about the EAP, told them I believed it would help and handed out EAP cards and brochures.

It was evident that the hate mail being sent to the MD was because certain employees were in the anger stage of the grieving cycle and were irrationally blaming the MD for the ex-employee's suicide.

Later I was informed that six of the ten employees had availed themselves of counselling and that all had benefited significantly from it.

One of those was the Operations Superintendent at the depot. He subsequently became an unofficial ambassador for the EAP at that depot and would address groups of employees about the benefits that he had personally gained from counselling. His totally authentic testimony was very powerful in influencing others to access the service.

CASE STUDY #3 — DEALING WITH DRUG ADDICTION

In a random drug test on a customer site, a well-regarded blue-collar employee tested positive for crystal meth. Like most companies, ours had a process for dealing with people who tested positive for alcohol or illicit drugs. However, an addiction to crystal meth was beyond what we would normally consider manageable. I set a meeting with the employee, his manager and the HSE Manager. In the meeting I told the employee that we wanted to help him but only if he wanted to help himself. He stated that he was committed to becoming "clean" so we referred him to counselling through our EAP. It took twelve sessions before the counsellor was satisfied that the employee could safely return to work.

This employee resumed his career and did not re-offend.

After his rehabilitation he offered to become the go-to person in the company for employees with addictions, and this did happen. Out of his strong sense of gratitude he also became a very positive advocate among the blue-collar people for counselling and for the company and its management. This depot had some very militant unionists so I have no doubt that the man's influence helped to change attitudes for the better.

AOD (alcohol and other drug) counselling through the EAP should be a mandatory part of a company's process for dealing with people caught with alcohol or illicit drugs in their system. It is also a way to introduce people to counselling if they've never experienced it and allow them to benefit in other areas of their lives.

In self-referred counselling, the average number of sessions is two or three. There is typically a mutual decision made between the counsellor and the recipient when enough sessions have taken place. With AOD counselling it needs to be the *counsellor's* decision as to when sufficient sessions have been done, as the counsellor needs to be convinced that the employee is committed to the process and has completed it. If the counsellor is unable to reach this view, they are expected to report it to the company.

CASE STUDY #4 — TRAUMA COUNSELLING AFTER A SERIOUS WORK ACCIDENT

An employee at a remote depot suffered life-threatening injuries in a work accident. For initial treatment he was taken by air ambulance to a population centre a couple of hours' flying time away then after being stabilised, he was flown by air ambulance to the state capital for an operation and treatment. He was placed in an induced coma and for over a week he was in intensive care as his life hung in the balance. In time he was brought out of the induced coma and began his recovery.

Immediately after being informed of the accident I contacted the employee's fiancée at her workplace, went to that location and stayed with her until her family arrived. The company's MD and I drove to the capital city airport at midnight that night to meet the employee's parents who had flown in from interstate.

As the worst accident in the company's history, this was a very traumatic event not only for the injured person but also for many others — the victim's immediate family and friends, his workmates, the wider population of the company and its management — including me.

The injured person's workmates were especially traumatised. One who was his best friend and housemate had been operating a piece of mobile equipment that was involved in the accident. Another, a young female office worker, was called on to administer first aid as other first aiders were out of the depot on jobs. Several of his workmates either witnessed the accident or were in the immediate vicinity when it happened.

After taking care of the injured employee's immediate medical needs I called the EAP provider, informed them of the accident and asked them to arrange trauma counselling. They elected to carry this out in the city rather than at the worksite and asked us to fly our people down from site so they could receive counselling away from the environment where the accident occurred.

All the people involved received counselling — family, workmates, immediate friends and company employees including management who were directly involved. Our action in arranging counselling was universally appreciated as a caring act. The accident brought to the fore a rift between the family of the injured person and the family of his fiancée; counselling was able to address this, with hopefully long-term benefit.

Through our approach to this accident we were able to demonstrate our compassion as a company. Many employees greatly appreciated it, including those who were not directly involved.

As I write, the injured person is on his way to making a full recovery. He married his fiancée and they have since had a child.

Threats to EAP success and ways to counter them

Threat one — falling victim to stereotypes

When promoting your EAP do not allow yourself to be put off by stereotypes. For example, people may believe that blue-collar males have a culture of not seeking assistance for their problems. This may make you less inclined to promote the service with this cohort. However, don't be misled; my experience is that when approached with understanding and compassion and a genuine desire to help, blue-collar males are very willing to receive and benefit from outside assistance.

Threat two — loss of momentum

Once established in a company, the EAP needs to be monitored for ongoing participation. The EAP provider normally supplies six-monthly reports covering participation rates and other data. At intervals you'll need to repeat the talks to workforce groups so that management's commitment to the process is regularly reinforced. Where possible, employees who have benefited from counselling can be called on to speak at safety meetings to keep everyone reminded of the benefits.

Threat three — the EAP provider is not satisfactory

Not all EAP providers are created equal. If you are setting up an EAP service, apart from comparing quotes it's good to interview the contenders' senior management so you can form an opinion of their company's abilities and genuineness. I have seen some providers become victims of their own success, being unable to provide counsellors when needed because they have too much demand for their services and too few people in the right locations.

Once the EAP is in place you need to be getting feedback regularly from people you have referred to the service to tell you how the provider is performing. The EAP provider is ethically bound not to disclose the identity of people who have self-referred so you should obtain feedback from people you know have been referred by other means. Feedback is essential so you know you're continuing to get a first-rate service. If you are receiving negative feedback you will need to contact the provider to reinforce your expectations and ask them to advise what remedial measures they will put in place to address your concerns. Then you will carry out follow-up checks to make sure the measures are effective.

Threat four — top management loses interest in the EAP process

To avoid this risk it is important to keep top management regularly updated on EAP progress and success. In addition to presenting the regular reports from the provider as to participation rates and percentage of issues brought to counselling that are personal as opposed to work-based, you should keep management informed of any stories of successful EAP intervention that those involved have given permission to publicise.

Create and actively promote a mentoring program

A mentor can be described as a wise and trusted guide. Mentoring can be defined as "a personal developmental relationship in which a more experienced or more knowledgeable person helps to guide a less experienced or less knowledgeable person" (Wikipedia).

The rewards to the mentees (the persons being mentored) can be immense, including being able to avoid, through the sage advice of their mentor, some of the more painful aspects of learning by trial and error. For a mentor there are few things more rewarding than watching the development, growing maturity and growing success of a person you are mentoring.

If your company doesn't already have a mentoring program, I strongly recommend you establish one.

A mentoring program serves the following functions:

► Fosters the development of employees, especially those who are new or inexperienced.

► Shows care for employees, company-wide and between mentor and mentee.

► Helps mentees to:

→ Overcome developmental obstacles and see a broader strategy for their lives.

→ Focus on their optimum career path.

→ Develop skills including life skills.

→ Promote a balance between the work and non-work aspects of their life.

▶ Improves employee retention. A well-run mentoring program is a big draw card.

The mentoring process has at its heart the care that the mentor has for the mentee and the keen interest they have in helping the mentee achieve their full potential. Setting up and actively promoting a mentoring program is a meaningful way to show care for your people.

Mentoring involves a relationship of trust. The mentee must trust their mentor and believe that their mentor cares about them and the outcomes they achieve. Mentoring conversations are strictly confidential; the mentee must feel confident that they can talk openly to their mentor and that the mentor will maintain confidentiality at all times. This relationship of trust is so important that in mentoring programs I have set up the mentee gets to choose who they want as their mentor then they approach that person and make the request. So if someone asks you to be their mentor, it is an honour and an affirmation of the trust that person has in you.

Because of the importance of trust in mentoring, there needs to be a culture of trust in the company.

Mentoring can be formal or informal. Informal mentoring is merely the supportive relationship that naturally grows between certain people in a company, for example inexperienced or newly hired technicians and their supervisors. Some people naturally see the need to be mentored and form relationships in the company or outside it with people they perceive as suitable mentors. Others can be introduced to mentoring and shown the benefits of it then will adopt it enthusiastically when it's offered as a formal program. Some people naturally mentor and don't need to be prompted.

A formal mentoring program is one set up and run by the company to look after internal mentoring. Mentoring programs work well if set up and run as follows.

▶ Someone at management level needs to be appointed to run the program and champion it, then given the time to do it properly. Appointing a person at this level shows the commitment of top management to the program.

▶ If there is no obvious candidate there can be a call for volunteers. The program manager should ideally be selected for their known commitment to mentoring, perhaps a person who already mentors unofficially in the company, and importantly someone who can engender trust. Such is the importance of trust in mentoring that picking as program manager a person not known for their trustworthiness would doom it from the start.

▶ The program manager develops the mentoring program, keeping all relevant people informed so employees are prompted to start thinking about their possible involvement as mentors or mentees.

- ▶ When the program is ready the program manager delivers a briefing to all employees. This briefing emphasises that people should select as their mentor only someone in whom they have a high level of trust.

- ▶ The program should be voluntary. Employees are informed about the program, educated about the potential benefits then given the option to participate.

- ▶ Having agreed to be mentored, the prospective mentee registers with the mentoring program manager. This is how the mentee makes their commitment to being in the program and it triggers the search for a mentor.

- ▶ The program manager advises the mentee how to go about choosing a mentor and what criteria to use in making the decision.

- ▶ The mentee decides whom they want as their mentor then approaches the person and asks.

- ▶ If the mentor agrees, they proceed. If not, for example because the mentor's time is already fully committed, the mentee must choose another mentor.

- ▶ The mentor need not be the person's supervisor or manager. People will sometimes default to selecting this person as their mentor because they believe that to do otherwise would be an insult. The manager or supervisor will normally be providing informal mentoring in addition to training so the program manager should guide the mentee to consider if another person would be better. An example of this, outside the business environment, is where an uncle or aunt mentors a nephew or niece. The mentoring relationship is helped because they have a trusted but non-parental relationship with the mentee.

Given the importance of trust in the mentoring relationship, the great thing about allowing mentees to choose whom they want as their mentor is that only people who are trusted will be chosen. I have seen this lead to painful self-reflection on the part of those who think they would make good mentors but are not asked. Through this reflection they may be motivated to question whether lack of trust has been a factor and if so be prompted to adopt a more trustworthy approach.

Agreeing to be mentored is a big decision. By doing it the mentee accepts the mentor into their life and agrees to share confidential and sometimes personal information with them. This is a further advantage of making the mentoring program voluntary as the mentee needs to be in a personal space where they are prepared to accept being mentored.

Agreeing to be a mentor is also a significant decision, carrying the commitment to allocate time for mentoring sessions and related preparations, take a keen interest in the mentee's achievements and maintain absolute confidentiality about the content of the sessions.

Mentoring sessions are normally an hour long and occur initially every two to three weeks. As the relationship builds and progress is made, the frequency of contact can be reduced to one session a month.

As an affirmation of the mentee's desire to continue

the process, the mentee is normally made responsible for approaching the mentor to set up each session.

Mentoring meetings should always be conducted face-to-face where possible. This allows the mentor to monitor the mentee's responses and body language so they can adjust the direction of the conversation.

E-mentoring over Skype or FaceTime can also work well; I have effectively mentored people in other countries by this means.

Normally the identity of mentors and mentees is not publicised. This reinforces the confidentiality of the mentoring process and helps to avoid any office political problems that could arise from a person resenting that someone other than them was invited to be a mentor.

The selection of a mentor need not be permanent. Each mentor brings different strengths to the process. At intervals of say six months, mentees should be invited to consider choosing a different mentor. This can be voluntary (a change of mentor only at the request of the mentee) or more structured in that the mentors are chosen only for a period of six months then the process of mentor selection begins afresh. A mentee may elect to continue with their existing mentor. Mentoring is a great experience for the mentor as well so having a structured changeover interval potentially gives more people a chance to be a mentor. It also gives mentors the opportunity to mentor different people and gives mentees the chance to experience mentoring from different mentors.

A mentoring relationship evolves as it goes along. Initially trust is built up on both sides as topics for discussion are agreed. The middle section is the main mentoring process. Gradually the mentor guides the mentee toward growing autonomy so there is no residual dependence on the mentor.

Prior to the first session, the mentee should prepare a list of items they wish to include in the sessions. Once mentoring begins, the mentor helps the mentee to prioritise these items. However, in case the mentee has not come well prepared — not unknown for people with little or no experience of being mentored — the mentor needs to have a list of items prepared to prompt the mentee. When mentoring is within a company, it's likely the mentor and mentee know one another so the mentor will already have identified at least some of the mentee's needs.

There needs to be mutual accountability between mentor and mentee. As mentor you will often set tasks for your mentee to accomplish before the next session. You need to keep track of these so you can check progress at the start of each session.

As with an EAP, you will need to promote your mentoring program actively if it's to survive and thrive. Once the program is established, one way you can promote it is to ask a mentee to speak at each monthly staff meeting to tell others how they've benefited from mentoring. A mentor could be asked to share their experience and tell how they've benefited. The program manager should also be active in encouraging employees who have not yet selected a mentor to do so.

Having a thriving mentoring program adds a significant dimension of care for your people.

Act to reduce unnecessary stress in the workplace

There will always be some stress in a workplace. It can be due to the ever-present need to control costs, tight deadlines, restructuring or the fear of restructuring, changes such as the introduction of new processes or systems and changes in management personnel. We cannot always control these stresses because they are part of business.

You may think that work-related stress is unavoidable in high-pressure environments such as call centres. There is some truth to this but from discussions I have had with call centre employees, the quality of leadership and management in the centre has a great influence over the degree to which this stress affects the employees.

However, many stresses in the workplace are avoidable. Unnecessary stresses are caused by factors such as a lack of documented processes leading to everything being done *ad hoc*, poor and unreliable decision-making by management, ongoing unresolved interpersonal conflicts, bullying and harassment, and poor planning leading to frantic and chaotic activity to meet deadlines.

People differ in their response to stressors. Some people are chronically stressed at work no matter how little stress there actually is, whereas others manage to remain calm even in the face of immense pressure.

As a caring leader you need to be monitoring your people's stress levels and taking action with anyone whose stress level you believe to be too high. What can you do? You can start by talking in confidence to the person. A burden shared is a burden halved. The person may open up and tell you what the source of their stress is if it isn't already obvious to you. You might get a shock. One employee I approached to discuss my concern about his stress level told me that recently, for the second time, his son had threatened to kill him.

The action you take will depend on the cause of the stress. If you approach an employee about their stress level, you're making a commitment to act if it is within your power. Doing nothing when you could do something is not an option. A suggestion to access the EAP can be very much appreciated. The stressed person may reveal that an issue in your department is the cause of the problem. If so, you'll need to take action.

Meditation can help to reduce people's stress levels. I encourage people to meditate. See the section on remaining calm.

There is one factor fundamental to lowering the general level of stress in the workplace. It has to do with how you manage. I have touched on this elsewhere. If you stagger from one crisis to the next, you and your people will lead working lives filled with stress and uncertainty. Your people will suffer more because they are a step further removed from control.

One manifestation of this is so-called 'Seagull Leadership' where a manager flaps in, defecates on everyone, then flaps away again. This phrase encapsulates the reactive and panicky style of leadership that causes so much stress to employees.

Place high importance on proactive leadership and management and your outcomes and your people's lives will be better.

Act immediately at the first signs of employee distress

You can very effectively show care for your people by being aware of and responding to changes in their attitude or behaviour that could indicate stress, work issues or personal problems. You should school your people to watch for these changes in their workmates too.

In some ways people resemble structures; if a bridge or a building is under stress and approaching a point of failure it will often give off distress signals such as creaks and groans. Visible cracks may appear. If we are alert to these signs, and in the case of a structure that may include fitting strain gauges to measure minute movements, we can intervene to save the structure from collapse.

People under stress respond similarly. They give off warning signs and if those around them are alert to these they can be recognised and we can intervene. Warning signs include:

- ▶ Unexplained changes in behaviour or attitude, for example becoming uncooperative.

- ▶ Changes in alcohol consumption such as a non-drinker or light drinker becoming a heavy drinker.

- ▶ Becoming withdrawn or less extroverted than usual.

- ▶ A normally patient and mild-mannered person becoming short-tempered.

- ▶ People dropping hints, for example dropping muttered negative comments into conversations. These are often a cry for help — an invitation to others to ask them what's wrong and how they can help.

My experience is that in such cases early intervention brings the greatest chance of success. If you delay, the opportunity to get people back on the rails can be lost. This is because people under stress or in crisis can be their own worst enemies. By manifesting difficult behaviour, they can alienate their workmates and supervisors. Eventually the person uses up their goodwill, and people around them lose motivation, so early intervention is vital.

As noted elsewhere, my recommendation is to respond to abnormal behaviour without delay. That is to say, if someone is behaving or responding abnormally, take them aside and ask them in confidence if there is a problem. More often than not a person who has a problem and who is invited by someone they trust to discuss the problem will do so with openness and a great sense of relief. Through an act of caring, their burden has been lifted and they have been given hope of finding a resolution. These people acknowledged they needed help and were just waiting for someone to offer it.

Not everyone can be helped. People in personal crisis sometimes need to leave their employment to deal with their problems. We can only recognise the above indications and offer assistance. People will appreciate this caring approach. Sometimes the person seeks to return to the company once they have resolved their issues. A caring approach makes it more likely they will want to do so. If they do return, they're likely to have a great sense of gratitude for your understanding and this will bond them tightly to the organisation.

Give your time to your people when they need it

Some leaders and managers are gun shy when it comes to engaging with their people and helping them with issues that are troubling them. This can be difficult for managers and supervisors who have insufficient understanding of the people side of leading, and lack confidence in their ability to help people deal with their personal challenges. Yet as a leader you can and must cultivate the ability. You will find it very rewarding.

Not all managers are tuned in to this. Let's look at the case of John who comes to the office of his manager Irene.

John: 'Hi Irene, I'm wondering if you can spare me a couple of minutes. I have a personal matter I need to discuss.'

Like many managers Irene is always busy and finds it a challenge to manage her time. She has a degree in a technical discipline and is justly proud of her reputation for technical expertise but during her course she received minimal training in leadership and people management. Irene is highly proficient technically, but is known in the company as someone who lacks people skills.

Irene is working feverishly on figures she needs to finish to meet a deadline. In her mind she has every justification for not taking the time to speak with John. Secretly — for she is proud of her reputation and not keen to have her lack of people skills further exposed — she is happy to have a quasi-legitimate reason not to engage with him.

Irene: 'Hi John, I'd like to help you, but I'm snowed under at the moment. Can you come back tomorrow?'

John: 'OK, no problem.'

John leaves the office. Irene glances at him as he walks out — is it her imagination or does his body language convey an air of defeat? Are his shoulders slumped? Is he slightly stooped? Irene continues her work, relieved that she was able to avoid engaging with John at least for the time being. However, John needed Irene's help then and there, not tomorrow. John's wife has just been diagnosed with a life-threatening illness requiring major surgery and John needed help to deal with his feelings and reassurance that he would be able to get time off when he needs it.

Let us review the consequences of Irene's action in sending John away:

► John is less likely or unlikely to approach Irene in future if he needs help.

► Irene missed an opportunity to show care for John and establish a standing in the workforce as a caring manager who can be relied on to lend a sympathetic ear when needed.

► John is seriously distressed and distracted by his personal problem. He may be so distracted that he is a danger to himself and others in the workplace and actually needs to take time off. By not engaging with him, Irene denied herself the opportunity to evaluate his mental state.

► John's disappointment was compounded because Irene did not set another time for them to meet. Suggesting "tomorrow" is too vague and implies she doesn't really want to engage.

If only Irene had known, she already had the tools she needed. All John wanted was her undivided attention for fifteen minutes and a sympathetic ear so he could pour out his troubles. That alone would have made him feel better. Any helpful advice or support Irene could offer, and hopefully she would have offered it, would have been a bonus. It's not "rocket surgery". This is a key aspect of engaging with your people. You don't need special skills to engage; you just need to do it!

Show that you value life balance

Some people talk of a work-life balance. This suggests that the balance is between work and life as if life is everything you do apart from work. I see it differently. I think of it as life balance. Work is part of life and it will benefit your people if you help to ensure their lives remain balanced between the work- and non-work parts.

As part of promoting a caring environment I encourage people to lead balanced lives. For example, if I consider a person is working such long hours that it could jeopardise their health or home life, I talk to them and together we look for ways to reduce their hours. I touched on the following in an earlier chapter. I joined a company as the head of Shared Services, encompassing five departments including HSE and Quality. On settling in I found that one man, admittedly a very capable man, held the portfolios of HSE Manager and Quality Manager. This was a company of some 450 people in the construction industry, so both these areas were intensely busy. This employee, to the evident satisfaction of the chief executive who was saving a manager's salary, was working fourteen hours a day to keep up. He was showing signs of burnout. So I told him I would be hiring a second manager for one of these departments and I gave him the choice of which department he would retain.

Monitor your people and take action if their lives are too far out of balance.

You should consider how well your own life is balanced between work- and non-work activities. Also you need to consider if your work time is taken up with busyness. If you are always frantically busy you may not be allocating enough time to sitting back and thinking strategically about your department. One of my most creative and fertile periods was at a time when I wasn't constantly flat out busy. I had time to reflect and come up with new ideas, some of which were world-beaters.

If you are working constantly at full stretch, consider whether you're delegating enough to your team members. If you delegate more, both you and your people stand to benefit.

Some people become obsessed with work. We have all heard stories of retired businesspeople who lament having missed all their children's important occasions — birthdays, school plays, sporting events etc., because they were always working. I knew a mature-age woman whose whole life revolved around her work. When a nine-day fortnight was introduced she was upset as she didn't know what she would do with the extra day off each second week. You can encourage a person like this to accept that she — and her work — would benefit if she undertook other activities and improved her life balance. Of course, it would be her choice; but you would show care by bringing the subject up with her in an under-standing way.

Introduce wellbeing activities

Introducing wellbeing activities for your people is a caring act.

There are many wellbeing activities you can introduce or encourage senior management to introduce, to improve your people's experience of employment.

▶ Give people the option to take one of their sick days as a wellness (leisure) day every three months. This rewards people who do not otherwise benefit from their sick leave entitlement. People still need to keep a certain number of sick days available at all times for actual illness.

▶ Organise quarterly staff outings.

▶ Set up subsidised memberships at a gymnasium local to the company to encourage people to keep fit.

▶ Set up a personal development library.

▶ Offer assistance to quit smoking.

▶ Set up an annual self-questionnaire for stress.

▶ Encourage meditation.

There are many other ways. Be creative!

Offer and actively promote an adult literacy program

It is easy to assume that adults are literate. This assumption may be unfounded. Equally it is easy to assume that people whose native language is not English can nonetheless speak and understand English acceptably well, particularly if they nod in apparent understanding when you speak to them. This assumption may also be incorrect. They may be fully literate in their native language but not in English.

People who remain illiterate into adulthood become very

adept at hiding the problem. They don't want the shame that comes from exposure.

My introduction to the issue of adult literacy came when, as HSE and Quality Director, I was dealing with a 49-year-old electrical engineer from the former Yugoslavia. It came to my notice that he was regarded as poor at taking instruction from his company supervisor and from client personnel on site. Others in the company were inclined to dismiss it as just being due to cultural differences however I could not accept that. He was required to take instruction as a normal part of his work, so I was compelled to investigate.

The man did not strike me as likely to be bloody-minded or rebellious. He was a mature and competent professional so I was sure there must be some other explanation.

We met. I asked him if he was reluctant to take instruction and he said he was not. I noticed that when I spoke he would nod as if he understood, but his expression stayed strangely blank. I began to suspect he was having difficulty understanding. I set him a simple test: I made a short, clear statement then asked him to repeat it back to me in his own words. He couldn't.

So the problem was revealed. Because I dealt with him in a caring and empathetic manner and restricted the number of people in the company who knew about it, the man didn't feel embarrassed or ashamed.

This engineer spent much of his working life out on site and had time to study in the evenings. We went together to a local bookshop that specialised in language training books and DVDs and I arranged for the company to purchase items for him.

You can imagine the gratitude this man had for what we had done. It later emerged that he and his wife had been socially isolated due to their limited English skills, so I hope and believe we helped to alleviate that as well.

Caring and your quality system

You can turn your quality system into a very effective marketing tool if you use it to show your customers that you care about and value their opinions.

My experience is that if you show care for your customers they will see it as a positive differentiator and are likely to favour you with more business.

In many companies, quality is treated as just a mechanistic function — audits to be done, procedures to be written and followed and documents to be controlled. As important as all this is, to do only this and related activities needed to comply with ISO 9001 or whatever standard you follow is to overlook that customers are people and inherently want to be cared for.

You can use your quality system to connect with your customers at a deeper level. You can achieve this by instituting Customer Satisfaction Questionnaires (CSQs) as part of your quality system.

A CSQ is a short questionnaire comprising twelve to fifteen questions. Here are some questions I typically use. They can be tailored to the work your company does.

- ▶ Were you satisfied with the work we did?

- ▶ Were you satisfied with the people we provided?

- ▶ Were you satisfied with the mobilisation of our people and equipment?

- ▶ Did you identify any additional training that our people needed?

- ▶ Did our people work safely?

- ▶ Were you satisfied with our report?

- ▶ Are we your preferred provider for this type of work?

- ▶ If not, what do we need to do to become your preferred provider?

- ▶ Did we exceed your expectations? If not, did we meet them?

- ▶ How could we improve so that in future we exceed your expectations?

- ▶ Will you use us in future?

- ▶ Is there any work we can quote on at present?

- ▶ Please give an overall rating for our work on this job, from 1 to 100 with 100 being the best.

- ▶ Do you have any other comments?

Where work is ongoing some of the above will be phrased in the present tense rather than the past tense.

The results of CSQs (the percentage ratings) should be plotted and presented as part of the monthly quality management report.

CSQs should be administered as follows.

- ▶ Do the CSQ with the customer manager who was responsible for your work on site and preferably the one who authorised the work and would authorise future work. Remember this is a marketing opportunity more than a quality matter.

- ▶ Do the CSQ over the phone, or face to face if you are making a visit to the customer site. Emailing a blank CSQ for the customer to fill in and send back takes away the personal element and makes it harder to probe further when the customer gives a negative response. Doing CSQs by phone works fine. Begin by saying to the customer:

  - → My name is ____ ____ and I am the ____ ____ (title) in our company.

  - → I've called to run through a Customer Satisfaction Questionnaire with you. The CSQ is part of our quality system and in it we ask a few questions about how satisfied you are with the work we did recently.

  - → The CSQ typically takes seven or eight minutes.

  - → Do you have time to do it now?

It's important to state how long the process takes. Most managers are busy and if they know a CSQ will take only a few minutes they'll often agree to do it on the spot, which saves you having to call back. A CSQ can be done in five minutes if the respondent gives only brief answers, however if they really get into the process and give detailed answers it can take fifteen minutes. Seven to eight minutes is a happy medium.

It's no good annoying the customer by trying to force the CSQ on them if it's not a convenient time. Ask them to suggest another time for you to call. If a call at another time is required make sure that you, not the respondent, are the one calling back, so the initiative stays with you. It can be awkward if the respondent says they'll call back and doesn't.

It works best to type the customer responses directly into the CSQ as they're being given so the form needs to be set up for this. Mention to the customer that they'll hear you typing in the background, so they don't hear typing and think you're doing something unrelated.

A management person should make the CSQ calls. The process is too valuable to demean it by having an admin person do it and an admin person will not be able to probe negative responses as effectively as a manager can. You can arrange for all CSQs to be done by the one person or better still they can be shared across the management team thereby reinforcing the collective responsibility for marketing and for quality.

Ensure CSQs are done at arm's length; managers should not do CSQs on their own jobs.

If during the CSQ the customer raises a concern about any aspect of the work, first probe the concern to get full details then commit to investigate it and to get back to the customer with the outcome of the investigation. Closing the loop is crucial to deriving full benefit from the CSQ process and demonstrating your commitment to continual improvement.

A CSQ should be done at the conclusion of each job. However, if your company does a large number of jobs each month, select a manageable number covering high value or potentially high value clients and do CSQs on these. Always do CSQs on jobs where you believe there are or have been problems.

When you have ongoing work with a customer, a CSQ every two to three months is sufficient. Normally you would do this with a different respondent each time or at least alternate two respondents so people are not irritated by the process and don't end up just repeating answers from the previous CSQ.

CSQs bring the following benefits to your company.

► You give yourself a legitimate opportunity to connect with your customers, not just for a sales call, at a time when you might not otherwise be in touch with them.

► You offer the customer value by giving them the chance to feed information back about your company's performance.

► You show care for the customer and validate them personally by seeking their opinion.

► You make clear your commitment to doing high quality work by asking customers the tough questions about any problems they've had with your work.

► You make it clear that you want to improve.

► You create an opportunity to make a commitment that you then keep, thereby building trust. That commitment is to investigate any problems or concerns raised and get back to the customer with the outcome and remedial actions taken.

▶ Providing feedback after the investigation is a further legitimate reason to connect with the customer and add value.

▶ Each positive customer contact provides an opportunity for the customer to advise you of work they need you to do.

Exercises

→ Do you view relations with your people through a lens of care?

→ Have you experienced how much more readily people accept an offer of help if they have acknowledged that they need help?

→ Does your company's chief executive make a personal commitment to care for employees?

→ Does your company have a formal set of values that were consultatively developed, are regularly workshopped, are universally understood and communicated to clients and suppliers as well as employees?

→ How effective are anti-bullying measures in your company?

Exercises

▸ Do you personally acknowledge that your people have a higher purpose and actively encourage them to strive to realise it?

▸ How effectively are accidents investigated in your company? Is there a robust system in place to implement post-investigation controls and monitor their effectiveness?

▸ Talk to a worker who has returned to duty after a work injury. Do they feel that the company cared well for them?

▸ Does your company monitor safety climate regularly? How good are the results?

▸ Does your company have an EAP? If so,

→ How effectively is it used?

→ Is it actively promoted?

→ What is the participation rate?

→ Do managers encourage people to access the EAP?

→ Are you aware of successful interventions of the EAP with your people?

Exercises

▶ Does your company have a mentoring program? If not, what can you do to get one started?

▶ How would you describe people's typical level of stress in your company?

▶ How do you respond if one of your people appears troubled or distressed?

▶ How do you handle requests from your people to speak in confidence with you?

▶ Is life balance valued in your company?

▶ Do you suspect that any of your people have literacy issues? How will you deal with this?

▶ Does your company's quality system incorporate CSQs? If not, discuss the workings and benefits of CSQs with the Quality Director or Quality Manager and recommend CSQs be introduced.

Chapter 15

How do you handle people who are trying to take advantage of you?

In my experience most people respond positively to being treated in the manner described in this book.

However not everyone does. Some see it as an opportunity to do less work or to pursue their own agendas that are not aligned with company's agenda. You cannot ignore such behaviour and you will need to deal with these people in a different way.

As a person's supervisor or manager you have a right to have your lawful instructions obeyed, including where these instructions are conveyed in the form of a request.

People who are determined to do as they wish can disguise it by being sycophantic toward you, thinking that by doing so they avoid arousing suspicion. These are the first people I am curious about as my approach of treating people as equals makes it clear that I do not wish or expect to be treated this way. Fortunately, "the truth is out there" and if a person is being deceptive they will not be able to maintain it indefinitely.

If certain people are still being obsequious once they get to know you it may be because they think it will provide the path of least resistance to their goals. It is simple enough to test a person whom you suspect of such duplicity — deny them what they want in some respect. If their mood changes instantly, for example if they become angry, you will know they are being disingenuous. The person whose motives are genuine may be disappointed at being denied something, but knowing you they will understand you made the decision for good reasons and will not be resentful. The person who is trying to fool you will be unmasked.

Those whom you cannot trust reveal themselves in other ways. For example, you ask someone to perform a task; they do not do it, then either offer no explanation or make some lame excuse.

It's likely that people whom you can trust, who are doing a great job and appreciate your leadership, will feel resentment toward those who try to take advantage. They feel aggrieved because they appreciate your trust and consider that the other person is not responding appropriately to the opportunities you are giving them. They will tell you directly what is going on or drop broad hints to arouse your curiosity.

Be careful how you respond. If you brush their concerns aside, your credibility and trust will be diminished with the person who brought the issue to you. You will need to respond, however before taking any action you need to verify that what has been reported is correct. When someone comes to you angry at a third party's behaviour it is easy to get caught up in the emotion. They are incensed, they expect you to be too and they expect you to leap into action. I know that at times I have fallen into this trap. Calm the situation so you can objectively unravel the threads and obtain supporting evidence. This also has the effect of showing the person who came to you that before taking action you will always test the information you receive.

Even people who are strongly loyal to you and strive to do their best do not achieve it every time. So despite the frustration you feel when something goes wrong, give the benefit of the doubt in the first instance.

If unacceptable behaviour occurs more than once this is an indicator that all is not well.

Once you establish there is a problem with a person, you need to consider how to deal with it.

Reacting to your feelings of anger and betrayal by reaching for a big stick in the form of disciplinary action may not be productive. It satisfies an understandable and very human inclination to get even; you feel resentment toward the individual because they are apparently taking advantage of you. Applying a disciplinary measure may be inappropriate if information you have based it on proves to be incorrect, and it may irretrievably fracture your relationship with that person.

You need to make a judgment about the person's motives. Sweep your side of the street first, for example by ensuring that the person fully understands any instructions you have given.

If all evidence points to a person behaving inappropriately you will need to discuss your concerns with them. Choose a time when you can do it without anger.

Their response will determine what you do next. If they show contrition you might accept this at first because it will soon be evident whether they are genuine.

As discussed elsewhere it may be that the person has some personal or work-related problem about which you know nothing. Give them an opportunity to reveal and discuss this so you can offer help.

If your approach is met with intransigence you will need to take a harder line. Subject to your company's disciplinary code you would normally start by writing to the person, copying in your Human Resources department, setting out your concerns and confirming the actions you propose to take as discussed in your meeting. Options include placing the person on a program to monitor and manage their performance.

Not everyone can be brought around. Perhaps the person would be better off working in another area of the company. Depending on the circumstances you may need to initiate a process of further disciplinary measures that would eventually lead to dismissal unless behaviour improves.

I find it difficult to hold trust for and suspicion about a person simultaneously. I start by trusting and in most cases this is justified. However, once my trust has been breached it is as if a switch has been flicked and it will take a lot for me to trust that person again. Of course, I do not discriminate against them but I feel differently about them.

Exercises

▶ Have you had experience of a team member or a peer who was trying to take advantage of you?

▶ Did the person try to disguise this?

▶ How did you deal with the issue?

▶ Did you achieve a successful outcome?

Chapter 16

Motivation

As leaders, part of our role is to motivate our people. Following the tenets of this book will foster high levels of motivation in your people.

We can distinguish between intrinsic and extrinsic motivators.

Intrinsic motivators come from within us; for example if we are passionate about something, we really enjoy doing it, we find it satisfying and fulfilling and we want to do our best at it. So choose your career carefully so that your passion for it will carry you along!

Extrinsic motivators are external and include appreciation, fear, financial reward, public acclaim and avoidance of adverse outcomes.

Appreciation and recognition can be effective motivators if genuinely given and not over-used. In a previous chapter you will have read the story about the female employee who told me that the appreciation I showed for her efforts made her want to do as much for me as possible.

However, there is a limit to the effectiveness of some external motivators; for example, if I receive an end-of-year cash bonus I will probably relate that to how much I'm earning. Research has shown that most people are not motivated by money beyond a certain point, so a cash bonus may not be an effective motivator. Conversely, if I deem the bonus too small it may act as a demotivator!

Fear as a motivator has limited value and is eventually damaging. It may produce short-term bursts of productivity, but it will destroy trust in the individuals who wield it.

You can significantly enhance motivation by removing sources of demotivation. In my experience most people naturally want to do their best, and they will, if as far as possible you remove obstacles. The best you can do is get out of their way by creating an environment where they have no impediment to doing their best. In this respect you can choose to see yourself as a support for and facilitator of what your people are trying to do.

Poor leaders and managers create, or do not work to remove, a trail of obstacles for their people. For example if systems, processes and procedures are poor or non-existent, people will become frustrated. For a time they will try to push through but eventually they'll become demotivated. Their justifiable view will be that management is responsible for providing suitable systems. I have often seen the demotivating effects of poor systems. In my management work I have always striven to provide my people with first-rate systems.

You cannot supervise people continuously. Most of the time they're working without oversight from you or others. So their motivation to put in the effort and attain the highest standards is critical.

As a leader you will occasionally encounter people who lack motivation. You should engage with them and find out why. This engagement is in itself a caring act.

Exercises

▶ Have you worked for a manager who led by fear? How did that affect you and the people around you?

▶ How do you rate the systems and processes with which you work?

Chapter 17

Lead and manage safety well

L eading and managing safety well is an excellent way to engender trust and to demonstrate how well you care for your people.

My experience, supported by research and the experience of others, is that people who feel well cared for achieve, among other things, better safety outcomes. Some research suggests that this is because employees who feel well cared for are more likely to follow the safety procedures that are designed to protect them (see the section "Safety climate foundational research" in Appendix I.) My take on it is that when an employer cares for their employees, the self-esteem of those employees improves (whether they realise it or not) and as a result the employees naturally want to take better care of themselves. This translates directly into safer behaviour and better safety outcomes.

First rate safety management means that:

▶ The company culture, emanating from the highest levels, openly declares safety to be the top priority.

▶ Management provides continuous visible commitment to safety.

▶ Risk management is thoroughly understood, universally practised, and maintains a focus on the critical risks.

▶ The company's HSE management plan is a living document.

▶ Safety procedures are developed consultatively then fully and consistently rolled out.

▶ The understanding, application and effectiveness of procedures that impact safety are regularly tested.

▶ Everyone is aware of the phenomenon of "normalisation of deviance" and is vigilant for manifestations of it (see the section below headed "Avoid a culture of blame").

▶ Reporting of hazards is actively encouraged. Identified hazards are promptly investigated, appropriate action is taken to control them, and outcomes are widely communicated.

▶ Safety incidents including near misses are thoroughly and impartially investigated, the root causes are identified and measures are implemented to prevent recurrence (see below).

▶ There is a strong commitment to meaningful auditing and to the correction of deficiencies found.

▶ Auditing is carried out at arm's length and never by people directly involved in or responsible for the activity being audited.

▶ The implications for safety of any proposed cost-cutting measures are carefully risk-assessed before changes are made.

▶ Strong HSE advisor support is provided.

Most safety legislation embodies a requirement for an organisation to exercise a "duty of care" toward its employees and other parties. Unfortunately this phrase is too often treated as safety-speak and just translated into procedures and mechanisms without any consideration of what it really means. What is the better way? Take duty of care literally and care for your people in the ways I have described!

Thoroughly investigate accidents, incidents and near misses

Every time an accident, incident or near miss occurs it must be investigated. Each time you lead or participate in an investigation you have an opportunity to show care and build trust with your workforce by doing the investigation thoroughly and impartially.

Those responsible for carrying out a safety investigation are often under pressure to complete it as soon as possible so 'normal' operations can resume. While there are understandable pressures to move things along, those who apply pressure to close out investigations quickly do not always understand the importance of doing them properly, and the consequences if they don't. If you succumb to this pressure you are likely to close out an investigation prematurely, before the root causes have been found. This will inevitably lead to a repeat of the unwanted event, perhaps with a much worse outcome.

A safety investigation has a certain natural rhythm. Initial enquiries yield evidence that must be checked and corroborated. As you probe further you identify more questions. Only when investigators are satisfied that the root causes have been identified and no significant questions remain unanswered can conclusions be drawn, remedial measures identified and implemented and the investigation closed out.

Employees often know when an investigation has been half-done and closed out prematurely. They usually know why. It destroys trust.

There is only one acceptable course of action: strive to ensure that all safety investigations for which you are responsible or in which you are involved are carried out thoroughly and to the highest standard.

Avoid a culture of blame

In organisations that are poorly led, when accidents happen there is a tendency to blame individuals rather than identify and correct the root causes that more often than not lie with the organisation itself. This blame destroys trust in the leadership and precludes any belief on employees' part that the leadership cares for them.

When an investigation is closed out prematurely and doesn't progress to finding the root causes, some causes must still be found. Too often, blame is placed on people. In most cases it is not justified.

As an example, why did the operator put his hand into the machine when it was running, to clear the blockage? Was he to blame? Superficially it's easy to blame him. He did something that was prohibited and was clearly wrong. But this machine had been prone to blockages for months. Everyone knew it including management, but no one bothered to find out why or to fix the problem. People had been putting their hands in several times a shift to clear blockages so eventually someone removed the guard and put it aside so they didn't have to unbolt it each time. Tampering with protective guarding is illegal. All the supervisors knew about it but everyone turned a blind eye. This operator was only doing what other operators did and what management, by failing to intervene, was seen to condone. The difference was that this operator's hand was mangled.

In his 2004 book "The Blame Machine: Why Human Error Causes Accidents", R. B. Whittingham asserts the following (p255):

Companies and/or industries which over-emphasise individual blame for human error, at the expense of correcting defective systems, are said to have a "blame culture". Such organisations have a number of characteristics in common. They tend to be secretive and lack openness cultivating an atmosphere where errors are swept under the carpet. Management decisions affecting staff tend to be taken without staff consultation and have the appearance of being arbitrary. The importance of people to the success of the organisation is not recognised or acknowledged by managers and as a result staff lack motivation. Due to the emphasis on blame when errors are made, staff will try to conceal their errors. They may work in a climate of fear and under high levels of stress. In such organisations, staff turnover is often high resulting in tasks being carried out by inexperienced workers. The factors which characterise a blame culture may in themselves increase the probability of errors being made.

The scenario in the above example plays out all too often. People like the machine operator are blamed — scapegoated — when it is actually the system that is at fault, when the failings are of leadership and management.

Put yourself in the position of a person who was scapegoated — blamed for something they did not do or blamed when the system was at fault. Think of the sense of injustice, hurt and powerlessness the person would feel. If you were responsible for scapegoating them, every time they saw you it would remind them. No wonder that for them, trusting you or feeling a sense of care from you would be impossible.

The above scenario was also a classic case of normalisation of deviance: people knew a hazard (the deviance) existed — that of an injury to an operator from placing his hand into the machine when it was running — but because the hazard didn't *immediately* lead to an accident it gradually became normalised, became "part of the furniture" and its significance as a hazard faded into the background. We can be lulled into a false sense of security about hazards because often they do not cause an accident when they first appear. However, given time and continued exposure to the hazard an accident is almost inevitable. Normalisation of deviance has been a fundamental contributor to many catastrophes, including the loss of the space shuttles Challenger (1986) and Columbia (2003).

Manage injured workers with care

We should always do our utmost to prevent workers from being injured. If an injury should occur, the way we manage the injured worker will have a profound effect on their recovery, and on their perception of the company and how well it cares for them.

Injured workers feel vulnerable. If they are initially unable to work, they're likely to be fearful about their long-term work prospects and the financial consequences of being unable to work or of having to accept lower-paying work because their injury prevents them from returning to their former duties and work cycle. People tend to take their current deprived situation and extrapolate it out to the long term whether this is justified or not. For example, if a person needed lengthy rehabilitation with regular physiotherapy they may no longer be able to work on a fly-in fly-out roster on a remote site and earn the big money.

If injured workers are away from the workplace for an extended period they feel cut off from their workmates. This feeling of isolation may lead to depression that slows or arrests recovery or in extreme cases may lead to thoughts of suicide.

We should aim to treat injured employees as we ourselves would want to be treated in that situation. So:

▶ Appoint an Injury Management Coordinator (IMC). In smaller companies this person will also wear other hats, however you must understand that if a worker is injured the IMC will need to give immediate priority to managing the injury. The IMC needs to be a person with knowledge of injury management, the maturity and compassion to deal appropriately with injured workers and an understanding of how an injured worker will be feeling.

▶ Ensure the IMC receives formal training.

▶ Create an injury response kit containing instructions, a checklist of actions and the necessary forms, and ensure kits are available to each supervisor and manager.

▶ Ensure the procedure calls for the injured person's manager or supervisor to accompany them to the hospital emergency department or the medical practitioner, provide support and ensure that availability of suitable alternative duties is conveyed to the practitioner.

▶ Train managers and supervisors in these procedures.

▶ Have the general manager or department head call the injured worker initially to check how they're doing and confirm that they're being well cared for. This manager should provide their mobile phone number and invite the injured person to call them at any time if they have concerns. This provides a commitment to good care, reassurance that the injured person is not alone if they need anything, and backup to the actions of the IMC.

▶ Ensure the IMC phones each injured worker once weekly to check on their state of mind and on how their recovery is progressing. The IMC should also provide their work mobile phone number to the injured worker.

▶ When phoning, the IMC needs to be aware of any signs that the injured worker is not faring well. If the worker:

→ Repeatedly cannot be contacted,

→ Speaks unusually slowly or in a low voice,

→ Is reluctant to speak about the matter and wants to break the conversation off prematurely,

→ Expresses undue pessimism, frustration or anger about their situation or

→ Expresses concern about the financial repercussions of being unable to work,

the IMC must escalate the situation to their manager so a further intervention can be made.

▶ If an injured worker cannot be contacted by phone do not assume that no news is good news — it often isn't. You'll need to try other methods. For example, call the next of kin, or if the next of kin is not available send an email if you have the employee's personal email address, or send a registered letter to their home asking them to call the IMC. This persistence shows that the company cares. Partners or next of kin do not necessarily think to contact the employer as they may assume the employee would prefer they didn't, or that the employer won't care. As an employer you have an obligation to manage your employees' injuries and as a caring employer you should be proactive.

- ► Typically, when contact is made with the partner or next of kin, they are happy to act as a go-between.

- ► Create a close working relationship with the workers' compensation manager of your company's insurance broker. This person will have contacts with rehabilitation providers and other relevant professionals and can help to smooth the path of any workers' compensation claim and educate the injured person about their rights.

- ► Ensure the IMC has appropriate support from management.

When injured workers are properly and compassionately managed, I have seen them go on to become unofficial ambassadors within the company, telling their workmates how well the company cared for them and spreading good vibes.

Also, if an injury is properly managed, the injured person's time off work is minimised, the cost of the claim is minimised, and the company's workers' compensation premiums are kept to a minimum.

Institute annual surveys of safety climate

Safety climate surveys provide a measure of the safety culture in your company as perceived by the people in the company. These surveys allow employees and management to express their views about the culture of safety in the company, how well safety is managed and how it could be improved.

Surveys are normally done online, though if access to the internet is not available they can be done with pen and paper. They're anonymous so participants can feel free to answer truthfully without fear of reprisal.

Getting your people to take the survey annually allows you to measure how perceptions are changing year to year and allows you to measure improvements in perception from measures you've taken. Personnel may differ between surveys; some people leave, and new people come in. So you can also check how well you're getting the safety message across to newcomers.

Equally you can benchmark your company's safety climate against those of other companies whose people have taken the exact same survey. When your survey results are outstandingly good (as many done by my people have been) you can use the results as a very effective marketing tool. The surveys provide objective evidence of how well your people believe safety is being managed.

Finally, safety climate surveys show your people that you care about them and that you are keen to know what they think, warts and all, so you can improve.

Exercises

▶ Have you worked in an organisation when a major accident occurred?

▶ What were the consequences for the injured person, for you and for others?

▶ Are accidents and near misses thoroughly investigated and properly closed out in your workplace?

▶ Have you worked in a culture where individuals were blamed when things went wrong? How did it feel?

▶ How well are injured workers managed in your organisation?

Chapter 18

Do *you* need to change?

I have demonstrated how important it is for your people to trust you and to know that you care for them and about them. To bring this about, perhaps you need to change.

If you are not the trusted and caring person described in the book, you will benefit from changing. Your first step is to acknowledge and accept the need to change. Then you can make the decision to change. Making the decision to change will give you the motivation to change. Are you ready to make that decision? The only person who can change you is you.

Is change possible for you?

The long-time chief executive of a global Australian-based company described himself as 'an archetypal command and control individual'. He populated the senior ranks of the company with similar people. One day he awoke and as he described it, saw the beauty in a flower for the first time. His epiphany extended to a realisation of how destructive his leadership style was and how many people he had burned or destroyed through it. He resolved to change.

Change for him was a monumental challenge because up

to that point he had the senior managers swimming in the same direction as him. Then he reversed direction. One can imagine that at first many of his colleagues viewed him with scepticism. He gradually taught the company a new way of working. Your challenge is unlikely to be as extreme so don't be put off!

You may believe that for you, change is too difficult or even impossible. You may feel it won't be worth the effort. You may believe the changed you will not be compatible with the needs of your job role. You may feel so trapped by people's expectations, created by the company's culture and your past behaviour that you feel compelled to continue as you have always been.

It has certainly been my experience that if you decide to change, you can. People may not immediately embrace the new you, but provided your actions remain totally consistent with your new paradigm they will come to see the changes as permanent and they'll accept that you have changed.

Your career has likely been full of change: different companies, different people, new locations, perhaps new countries, new skills and new responsibilities. You're already adept at change.

For me, changing was absolutely worth the effort. I didn't do it all at once and that made it easier. The positive results I obtained at each stage spurred my motivation. The more I changed the easier it became to change further.

As you change, you and your team are likely to perform better and be more productive. You still have whatever hard edge you need to deal with certain situations. The behaviour of the changed you will be less likely to generate problems so your path will be smoother.

Depending on how different you are after you change, you may surprise some people. Give them time — they'll adjust!

The process of changing

As you begin the process of changing you have two big advantages: you know you need to change, and with this book you have the tools.

The exercises at the end of each chapter or section are designed to help you recognise the need for change and to guide you in how to go about it. Practise these until you feel comfortable.

Take as an example making amends. Make amends to one person for a minor matter then review how it went. If necessary, adjust your approach before you do it again. Each time you make amends it gets easier and feels less foreign. Of course, in time you'll need to do it less often because you won't be wronging people.

If you have not been accustomed to making amends you may think others will perceive you as weak. In fact, making amends demonstrates your strength because although it is not easy, it is right. You will win people over. The positive responses you'll get will encourage you to keep going.

Once you are doing things the new way because you feel it, not just think it, you can say that you have truly changed.

Exercises

- ▶ Search your deepest self and draw a conclusion as to whether you need to change.

- ▶ List, in priority order, those aspects of yourself that you believe are most in need of change.

- ▶ For each item, make a plan as to how you will initiate that change.

- ▶ Start to carry out your plan, one area at a time.

- ▶ After each change, evaluate the process and results.

Chapter 19

How you and your company will benefit

E xpect a payback at many levels from application of the principles and practices in this book. Here are some of the benefits you are likely to see.

Better leadership

You are likely to find that your leadership is more effective when you apply these principles. For example, when your people feel empowered, trusted and well cared for they are more likely to take ownership of issues and try to solve them. If they cannot solve a problem, they know that in you they have an empathetic leader who will help them work through the problem or support its resolution in other ways without blaming them if something has gone wrong.

Your team will be on the lookout for problems you need to know about and will tell you so you can nip issues in the bud. Your people effectively become an extension of you. They know you support them, so they support you and your aims. This helps you to manage proactively and it breeds success.

Greater harmony and less tension in the workplace

If you apply these principles and minister appropriately to your people, they will have a sense of contentment and motivation that will make their work self-sustaining and promote a harmonious workplace.

Of course, there will be occasional interpersonal disputes and tensions you'll need to handle. If you deal with these expeditiously and justly you will strengthen your relationships.

Better employee retention

Employee turnover (employees leaving and having to be replaced) is costly to business; employers generally prefer to minimise turnover.

Turnover is costly for many reasons, such as:

▶ Replacement employees take time to get up to speed. In the interim it can be difficult to maintain standards, and existing employees and managers may find themselves having to spend time plugging the gaps.

▶ All too often it is the better employees who leave, because it is they who are more readily employable elsewhere, so the overall standard of the remaining employees goes down.

▶ Each time an experienced employee leaves there is the risk that corporate memory will be lost. This risk is generally highest when long-term employees leave.

▶ There can be considerable costs entailed in sourc-
ing replacement employees.

In my experience, employee turnover can be minimised
by applying the principles in this book.

There are many reasons that people leave their employment. I categorise these loosely as positive or negative reasons.

Positive reasons are those where the employee perceives a
benefit in leaving. Such reasons include receiving a significant
outside job offer that goes well beyond what you could offer,
changes to family commitments, seeking to broaden their
experience, taking a sabbatical or downsizing their career.
In this case the employee's departure does not reflect a bad
experience of employment.

Negative reasons are where the employee has no positive
reason to leave and would prefer to stay, were it not for factors
in their employment that cause them to leave.

Extensive research has been conducted into these negative
reasons. The commonly reached conclusions are that:

▶ People leave managers, not companies. Turnover is
very much a manager issue.

▶ Employees that leave:

→ Lack trust in management.

→ Feel undervalued and underutilised.

→ Lack autonomy.

→ Lack a challenge.

→ Are disrespected or demeaned.

→ Perceive the corporate culture as negative.

Managers can exert a strong influence over many of these factors.

If you lead your employees in accordance with the principles in this book, you remove the biggest potential reason for them wanting to leave: you.

Experience suggests that whilst money is an important motivator, people who are led according to these principles will decline much more lucrative outside offers because they so value the way you lead and the culture you have created. I have certainly observed this; a young electrical technician told me that he had declined an offer to work with another company on a fly-in fly-out roster to a remote mine site for more than twice the salary he was receiving with our company, because he placed such a high value on working in our culture.

Fewer industrial relations problems

To varying degrees, people want and need power, control and influence in and over their lives. Employees can feel deprived of these by the actions of their manager. When people are managed in ways that deny them a sense of control or influence their needs do not go away but are expressed in other ways. For example, these needs can be expressed through being an active member of a union, if one exists for the workplace. Unions give a voice to people who might otherwise lack a voice.

In saying this I am not making a statement in support of

unions, just recognising that people who feel deprived of a voice may see merit in belonging to a union.

As a leader applying the practices in this book, you will no doubt be treating your people justly and fairly, empowering them and giving them the voice that we all need and deserve. As a workforce they are more likely to be contented because you are not providing reasons for them to be discontented. They may still want to belong to a union, but you won't be giving them any reason to turn to the union for assistance.

Industrial problems can be driven by union ideology. This situation may at first appear unlikely to respond to the application of these principles because it is not being driven directly by management deficiencies. My experience however, is that as a leader your individual approach can make a big difference.

One of my roles was as an HSE manager in a heavily unionised environment on the Australian waterfront. Ideology — specifically the union's belief that its worldview should dominate the nation's politics — drove much of the industrial pressure on the site. A related driver was that some years earlier this union had been involved in a bitter struggle with the same employer in which the latter tried unsuccessfully to crush it. As you can imagine, when I worked for the company there was very little trust from the union leadership or the members as they believed the employer could try to stamp them out again at any time.

I was aware of all this when I joined but I decided to ignore it and just carry on doing what I customarily did.

From the beginning I reached out to the workers in a way that none of the other senior managers did. I think the other managers were too steeped in the psychology of chronic, bitter, management-versus-worker struggle and as a result made little headway. In fact, by being overly assertive or aggressive they just got the workers' backs up.

At the outset I made my trademark brief statement of personal care and commitment, delivering it to each shift group at pre-start meetings. I did this with four groups to ensure I caught everyone. By making this statement I allowed people to see inside me and to understand what was important to me. This is one way that using the principles in this book can set you apart; you are constantly reaching out to people rather than treating management as an arm's-length process with no personal involvement or empathy on your part.

This role was just a six-week assignment. Despite the short time and having many intractable operational problems to solve I made significant headway with these employees and their level of trust. Some of the workers came to me in confidence and told me that despite all the past bad feeling between them and the company they wanted to make the relationship work. So my conclusion is that few situations, perhaps no situations, are beyond hope.

If you empower your people, they will have less reason to seek power in other ways that may be detrimental to you and the company.

Resentment also plays a part; if you give your people no reason to resent you, they won't have a need to express resentment by being uncooperative or by stirring the industrial pot. See the chapter on resentment.

Better customer relations

Have you ever phoned a company to make an enquiry or place an order and had the person on the other end of the line unload to you about all their woes in the company? This has happened to me many times. A person doesn't always unload at the beginning of the call though I have known it to happen. However, during the conversation, perhaps after you notice something seems to be amiss and you ask, the bad news comes tumbling out.

What this tells me is that if the customer service staff — the public face of the company — are so resentful and disgruntled, there must be big problems with the company, its culture and management. If you were the caller would you want to do business with this company?

Employees who are content and empowered deal more effectively with customers. They're more likely to be proactive in responding to queries and going the extra mile to ensure customers are satisfied.

Personal rewards

You can see from the many stories I have told how rewarding my working life became once I learned to apply these principles. I treasure memories of the many positive experiences I have had and continue to have because I am trusted and known for caring about my people.

These rewards are just one dimension. Companies need people who lead this way because these people get better results. So your career will benefit. You will come to see the role you're in as more sustainable so you're more likely to stay and reap the full rewards of your work.

Exercises

▶ Evaluate your workplace in terms of the benefits achievable from applying the techniques in this book.

Appendix I

Evidence for the benefits of trustworthiness and caring

Evidence has surfaced in many places about the benefits that a trustworthy and caring leadership can generate in a company.

In some cases, the evidence came to light when researchers were looking for other things such as sources of excellence.

Some of what follows deals with the connection between feeling well cared for and achieving better safety outcomes.

Here is a selection of findings and references. It is not intended as a rigorous or exhaustive listing of the evidence, merely a taster from a number of disparate sources over time that support the connection.

Excerpt from "Building Trust: OHS Management in the (Australian) Mining Industry"

Authored by Neil Gunningham and Darren Sinclair, The National Research Centre for OHS Regulation, Australian National University. February 2012.

This working paper considered the influence that the level of trust between the various layers of management and the workforce had on the culture of a range of mining companies and the Occupational Health and Safety (OHS) outcomes the employees of these companies achieved. As such, its findings are directly relevant to one of the themes of this book. It is striking, but no surprise, that the research found safety outcomes were closely related to trust.

Following are selected quotes from the paper. The researchers sampled ten coalmining sites in three separate companies, in two Australian jurisdictions (New South Wales and Queensland). In order to sharpen contrasting experiences, those mines [whose results] were located close to the middle of the OHS performance spectrum were excluded from the study.

'Trust has been identified as important in facilitating improved outcomes in work health and safety through improved communication, cooperation, acceptance of decisions, knowledge sharing, organisational functioning, and other means. Trust (and mistrust) is a particular concern in the Australian mining industry.' (p3)

'Our findings suggested that without trust, workers treated almost all corporate management safety initiatives with suspicion and refused to buy into them.' (p8)

'Our research revealed the attitude of mine management to be particularly important because, as numerous workers and middle managers told us, the level of safety that a mine achieves, is in very large part the level that the "boss" wants.' (p9)

A quote appears in the paper from Pitzer's 1999 cultural survey of the Australian mining industry. One of Pitzer's most important findings was that: 'The "value" of "care about employees" that underpins the achievement of a positive safety culture seems lacking in the industry... the pervasive message employees connect with is that management does not "value" employees.' (p9)

A comment about the influence of management structure on the issue of trust (p13): 'Certainly, in those mines that had not pursued flatter management structures, hostility and mistrust between management and workers was considerably more evident.'

The paper quotes Conchie et al (2006, 1101) who aver that 'Engaging employees in decision-making not only increases trust in management... but also promotes within employees the perceptions that they are trusted by management. In turn these perceptions increase the personal responsibility that employees take for safety and safe behaviour. However, our own findings were particularly striking in this regard'. (p14)

'...some high OHS performing mines have achieved good levels of communication by working with and through the local union representatives, and this approach has often served to dissipate mistrust between workers and management.' (p16)

In their conclusion the researchers state: 'There is growing evidence that the effectiveness of many management tools, including OHS management systems, is heavily dependent on the culture into which they are received and that, in this respect, the presence of mistrust has a particularly potent capacity to undermine them. Indeed, in many circumstances, building trust is essential to the effectiveness of OHS management initiatives.' (p20)

Excerpt from "Psychology Today" website

The Unexpected Benefits of Compassion for Business: **Compassionate workplaces — good for employees AND the corporate bottom line.**
Published on April 22, 2013 by Emma M. Seppälä, Ph.D. in "Feeling It."

http://www.psychologytoday.com/blog/feeling-it/201304/ the-unexpected-benefits-compassion-business

Managers often mistakenly think that putting pressure on employees will increase performance. What it does increase is stress — and research has shown that high levels of stress carry a number of costs to employers and employees alike.

Stress brings high health care and turnover costs. In a study of employees from various companies, health care expenditures for employees with high levels of stress were 46 per cent greater than at similar companies without high levels of stress. In particular, workplace stress has been linked to coronary heart disease in retrospective (observing past patterns) and prospective (predicting future patterns) studies. Then there's the impact on turnover: 52 per cent of employees report that workplace stress has led them to look for a new job, decline a promotion, or leave a job.

But there's a different way. A new field of research is suggesting that when companies promote an ethic of compassion rather than a culture of stress, they may not only see a happier workplace but also an improved bottom line.

Consider the important—but often overlooked—issue of workplace culture. Whereas a lack of bonding within the workplace has been shown to increase psychological distress, positive social interactions at work have been shown to boost employee health—for example, by lowering heart rate and blood pressure, and by strengthening the immune system.

Happy employees also make for a more congenial workplace and improved customer service. Employees in positive moods are more willing to help peers and to provide customer service of their own accord. What's more, compassionate, friendly, and supportive co-workers tend to build higher-quality relationships with others at work. In doing so, they boost co-workers' productivity levels and increase co-workers' feelings of social connection, as well as their commitment to the workplace and their levels of engagement with their job. Given the costs of health care, employee turnover and poor customer service, we can understand how compassion might very well have a positive impact not only on employee health and wellbeing but also on the overall financial success of a workplace.

So why does compassion provide such a boost to employee well-being? One reason may be its impact on social connection. Research by Ed Diener and Martin Seligman suggests that connecting with others in a meaningful way helps us enjoy better mental and physical health and speeds up recovery from disease; research by Stephanie Brown at Stonybrook University has shown that it may even lengthen our life.

Despite this research, managers may shy away from compassion for fear of appearing weak. Yet history is filled with leaders who were highly compassionate and very powerful—Mother Teresa, Martin Luther King, and Desmond Tutu, to name a few. They were such strong and inspiring leaders that people would drop everything to *follow them. Wouldn't any manager wish for that kind of loyalty and commitment?*

Support for this view comes from research by Jonathan Haidt at New York University. His research shows that seeing someone help another person creates a heightened state of wellbeing that he calls "elevation". Not only do we feel elevation when we watch a compassionate act, but we are then more likely to act with compassion ourselves.

When Haidt and his colleagues applied his research to a business setting, he found that when leaders were fair and self-sacrificing, their employees would experience elevation. As a consequence, they felt more loyal and committed and were more likely to act in a helpful and friendly way with other employees for no particular reason. In other words, if a manager is service-oriented and ethical, he is more likely to make his employees follow suit and to increase their commitment to him or her.

Elevation may even be a driving force behind creating a culture of compassion and kindness, whether in a workplace or in society at large. Social scientists James Fowler of UC San Diego and Nicolas Christakis of Harvard have demonstrated that helping is contagious: acts of generosity, compassion, and kindness beget more generosity in a chain reaction of goodness. This is how culture is formed. Isn't that the kind of workplace culture you would want to work in or lead?

Research on compassion is setting a new tone for the workplace and management culture. But this field is still new. Scientists are exploring the most effective ways to foster compassion in the workplace, and to help these best practices spread across companies.

I am struck by the last sentence in the above. I trust that from reading this book you have come to understand that whilst a scientific approach may be needed to promulgate these practices across companies, compassion is a very personal thing that is spread by the attitudes and behaviour of individuals.

Excerpt from "Leaders in Australia", the Australian Cultural Imprint for Leadership, 1996

Perhaps the most significant single observation from the study is that leaders care for their followers.

> *Success (in building these bridges) is heavily dependent on a leader's capacity to be seen to identify with, and respond to, the emotional needs of his or her followers. To do this leaders must be prepared to show something of their own emotions and the depth of the care they have for their followers' wellbeing.*
>
> *Followers learn more readily, accept directions, and at the same time feel more secure, when their leader displays this concern and commitment.*

Excerpts from ACIRRT "Simply the best workplaces in Australia": University of Sydney 2003

ACIRRT is the Australian Centre for Industrial Relations Research and Training. It is now known as The Workplace

Research Centre (WRC). It is one of Australia's leading research companies on work and employment and is based at the University of Sydney.

In this study eight excellent workplaces were compared with eight good workplaces. The study found:

- Fifteen key drivers of excellence.

- That mutual trust, respect, self-worth and recognition are paramount.

- That leaders must be aware of the impact of their behaviour and constantly renew and reaffirm relationships.

- That regarding safety: 'People understood they were part of a company that placed priority on (their) health and safety'.

- Also regarding safety: 'Feeling safe and secure comes from confidence, knowledge, training and particularly the experience of knowing that other people care for your well-being'.

Safety climate foundational research

This research was undertaken in Western Australia in 1998 to establish a multi-industry measure of safety climate. A structured qualitative analysis was carried out using direct input from safety experts and managers across a range of industries to determine the factors that distinguish positive and negative safety environments. Items from that analysis were then subject to rigorous statistical validation. The research showed that:

- not only is "care for employees" an important component of a positive safety climate, but also

- positive perceptions about the extent to which a company genuinely cares for its employees is fundamental for employees to engage with other elements of the safety systems that are designed to protect them.

This research led directly to development of the Safety Climate Index survey detailed elsewhere in the book.

Understanding Individual Compassion in Organisations: The Role of Appraisals and Psychological Flexibility

Associate Professor Paul W. B. Atkins (Australian National University) and Professor Sharon Parker (University of Western Australia), October 2012.

Abstract: To enhance compassion in companies, the processes by which compassion can be enhanced in individuals must be understood. We develop an expanded model of the components of compassionate responding that includes noticing, appraising, feeling, and acting. Using this model, we propose that psychological flexibility (mindfulness combined with values-directed action) contributes to enhancing the perceptual, cognitive, affective, and behavioural aspects of compassion. Specifically, mindfulness processes support the capacity to be compassionate while values processes motivate effort to engage in compassionate action. Training in psychological flexibility should be considered as one element of programs designed to increase organisational compassion.

An article published in *The Sunday Times* of Western Australia in November 2013 summarised the findings of this research paper. The article stated in part:

▶ Managers should be trained to be compassionate because too many are (too) preoccupied with their own feelings to notice an employee suffering.

▶ The research found that a lack of compassion in the workplace has become far too common.

▶ Managers were more likely to be in tune to (sic) other people's feelings if they were able to step back from their own thoughts.

▶ Quoting from the research, 'Compassionate behaviour in companies is associated with increased helping, trust, support and cooperation. But individuals can be too preoccupied with their own feelings, or too emotionally unregulated, to even notice the suffering of another, let alone do something about it'.

Appendix II

Bureau Gravitas
— a case study in caring

It is not only employees who benefit from being cared for. I now tell the story of a business I ran with two others between July 2001 and January 2005 and whose success was built on caring.

In June 1999 I was taken on to manage a joint venture (JV) between a large Canadian company and an even larger US company. The objective of the JV was to market off-road tyres and tyre management to the mining industry in the six north-western states of America.

It took six months to obtain my US visa and I spent the latter half of 1999 in Canada waiting for the visa, which finally arrived in January 2000.

My wife and I decided to come back to Australia in December 1999 to spend the millennium New Year's Eve with our children there.

Early in January 2000 I received a call from the Canadian company telling me that the major supplier to the JV had pulled out, so the JV was no longer viable and was to be abandoned. My visa was specific to the JV so with the JV wound up I had no right to work in the US. I had no right to work in Canada so I no longer had a job.

I was back in Australia and unemployed.

The year 2000 was not a good time to be a mature-age person seeking work in Australia. The economy was in recession and people were being laid off. In the rush to trim numbers, the merits of having an age-balanced workforce were not appreciated and mature-age people were being laid off in preference to other age groups.

During the next eighteen months I searched for work and took various training courses. One such course, in March of 2001, sought to train participants in how to seek work. On the course I met two men in a similar situation to me. One was a participant and the other was the course facilitator.

We soon realised that we were kindred spirits and we began to meet regularly, at first for mutual support and to share experiences then increasingly to plan our future.

Our shared view rapidly became that mature-age people like us had a vast amount to offer to employers and society. We decided that we should start a business to show others in our situation that they too had value and that they should continue to seek work and strive to have their value recognised.

We named our business Bureau Gravitas. Bureau signified a business offering services and Gravitas denoted one of the values that mature-age people bring: 'Gravitas — a serious and impressive attitude or way of behaving'.

We believed that the government-sponsored process for assisting jobseekers was unwittingly disempowering them. For example, the process mandated that jobseekers had to make a certain number of job applications per two-week period or have their benefits cut off. This focused people on the number of applications made rather than on the quality of the applications or on whether they actually wanted the jobs for which they were applying. They were being squeezed to apply for jobs irrespective of whether they wanted a particular role or were likely to succeed at it. This pressure was at odds with the need for people to develop a passion for a particular role and to write a convincing application in pursuit of it.

Also the benefits process itself was quite threatening. Jobseekers would periodically receive official letters warning of the dire consequences of making too few job applications or of giving false or misleading information. Of course, such communications are necessary for the small minority who don't do the right thing but for the majority they add to the sense of disempowerment.

The most significant shortcoming of the government approach was that it did not address the way job seekers were feeling about themselves. The process required jobseekers to apply for jobs at a time in their lives when they felt least able to succeed at job search.

Many mature-age jobseekers were the heads of their families and had been the sole or principal breadwinner until losing their job. Their inability to deliver brought on low self-esteem, a deep sense of shame and in many cases depression, all of which interfered with their ability to obtain work. A sense of disempowerment and often hopelessness permeated every facet of their job search. Examples include the following:

▶ Drafting their resume. A jobseeker who feels unworthy unintentionally distorts their resume by downplaying or failing to emphasise their accomplishments and presenting themselves in a less favourable light than they deserve.

▶ Selecting jobs for which to apply. A disempowered jobseeker shies away from applying for jobs they could actually do, believing (with their distorted view of themselves) that the job would be beyond them and the employer would realise this so an application would be futile.

▶ Writing letters of application. It is possible to judge a jobseeker's level of self-belief from how they phrase their letter of application. Disempowered jobseekers write unconvincing letters of application because their true view of themselves shows through.

▶ Performance at interview. In the unlikely event that they gain an interview, a jobseeker who feels disempowered and unworthy is unlikely to be convincing when interviewed. Their deepest belief is that they cannot do the job and the interviewer is likely to detect this.

Further, out of a sense of shame the disempowered jobseeker loses touch with their professional network at the very time they need it most. Bureau Gravitas had many conversations with government officials about this phenomenon because they had observed it but could not understand the reasons for it.

Between April and June 2001, we developed what we called our Personal Empowerment Program. In developing the program, we built in our understanding of how our program participants were feeling and what they most needed, which was to feel cared for and valued. Our groups comprised six to twelve people and each program ran for six weeks with one two-hour session per week. We began to deliver the program to paying customers in July 2001.

A number of sources fed us participants for groups:

▶ Job Networks — the Federal government-funded bodies charged with assisting jobseekers to find work and with monitoring their job search activities to ensure they continue to be eligible to receive jobseeker benefits.

▶ Various state government bodies that provide jobseeker support through courses.

▶ The Federal government body responsible for rehabilitating injured people such as victims of car accidents or industrial accidents and bringing them back into the workforce.

We also put together composite groups from these and other sources when we had insufficient participants from any one source to make up a group. Typically, two Bureau Gravitas directors facilitated each program.

The program worked as follows.

▶ We introduced ourselves. We explained our personal backgrounds, how we came to create Bureau Gravitas and how we selected the company name.

▶ The participants gave their background and aspirations. Each person was given a few minutes to do this.

▶ We explained how people were likely to be feeling and to be affected by their joblessness and invited the participants to relate their personal experiences.

▶ We provided arguments in favour of going after

jobs that the jobseekers actually wanted and gave them methodologies for deciding this. Of course we emphasised that participants needed at all times to comply with government requirements in order to continue receiving benefits.

▶ We taught the participants techniques for writing applications and succeeding at interview.

Most of all we made it clear that we personally cared about each participant and we were personally involved and interested in their progress.

Our program was highly successful. With our major client we kept records of outcomes; we found that within six months of completing the program 78% of participants had returned to meaningful activity. For the vast majority this meant paid work. That was despite most of our participants having come from the too-hard basket of the agencies that referred them. Most participants were long-term unemployed whose prospects of obtaining work were poor. Overall our groups comprised equal numbers of men and women.

Over the three and a half years we ran the program, we put close to a thousand participants through. Eventually a mining boom that gained momentum in the state of Western Australia in 2004 sucked up jobseekers irrespective of age. Of course, this demonstrated that mature-age people were worth employing after all! Our business ran out of clients and we closed in January 2005.

Every participant in the program had a story worth telling. Here are some.

One of our participants was the patriarch of a Greek family and had been the breadwinner until he lost his job. He was suffering badly from the shame of not being able to deliver and he felt unable to share this with his family. We suggested he call them together and tell them how he was feeling. He took our advice. He and his family had a very frank and emotional bonding session and it enabled him to make a fresh start with his job search, supported by his family's understanding.

Many program participants — we estimated around half — were suffering from depression, mostly undiagnosed. Two participants in one group, a husband and wife, were particularly badly affected. As the wife began to tell her story to the group, she burst into tears and sobbed inconsolably for some minutes. The facilitators and the group offered understanding and support. This mutual support was a strong feature of all our groups and happened spontaneously. We firmly believe that this woman was shedding tears of relief because she had finally found people to care about her and support her through the process. She felt hope that with everyone's support she could rescue herself from the depths of despair. Her husband was by her side and very supportive but the practical help he had been able to give her was limited because he was in the same position as her and wrestling with his own demons.

One of our participants, that we know of, was saved from committing suicide through his involvement in the program. His partner told us of this. The program gave him hope that by his own efforts he could bring an end to his jobless suffering. In fact, he became a program facilitator for Bureau Gravitas then found meaningful work after the company was wound up.

My two colleagues and I found our work at Bureau Gravitas highly rewarding and we felt honoured to have had the opportunity to help so many people in their hour of need.

Appendix III

Sir Ernest Shackleton — a caring hero

Sir Ernest Shackleton was a famous Antarctic explorer. He was also an outstandingly caring leader and a hero of mine for this and other reasons.

Born in County Kildare Ireland on 1 February 1874 he joined the British Merchant Navy in 1890. An adventurer, he volunteered for Robert Falcon Scott's ("Scott of the Antarctic") Antarctic expedition in 1901 and man hauling their sledges, Scott, Shackleton and Dr Edward Wilson reached latitude 82° 17' south, only 745 statute miles from the South Pole and further south than any human had been.

Shackleton contracted scurvy on the march to the pole and was eventually invalided home. He recovered and his thirst for Antarctic adventure and accomplishment remained unquenched.

He went south with Scott again in 1909 and this time came within 100 statute miles of the pole before having to turn back. On this expedition he showed that trait of caring for his men that would be one of his hallmarks and his legacies. The following is drawn from Caroline Alexander's excellent book *The Endurance* (p13). The men were man hauling their heavy sledges on limited, almost starvation, rations.

Early in his career, Shackleton became known as a leader who put his men first. This inspired unshakable confidence in his decisions, as well as tenacious loyalty. During the march back from 88° south, one of Shackleton's three companions, Frank Wild, who had not begun the expedition as a great admirer of Shackleton, recorded in his diary an incident that changed his mind forever. Following an inadequate meal of pemmican (a concentrated mixture of fat and protein) and pony meat on the night of January 31, 1909, Shackleton had privately forced upon Wild one of his own biscuits from the four that he, like the others, was rationed daily.

"I do not suppose that anyone else in the world can thoroughly realise how much generosity and sympathy was shown by this," Wild wrote underlining his words. "I DO (and) by GOD I shall never forget it. Thousands of pounds would not have bought that one biscuit."

Such is the enduring power of one caring act.

In 1914 Shackleton mounted his own expedition with the aim of being the first to walk across Antarctica. Frank Wild was his second-in-command. The expedition set out from England on the aptly named *Endurance* on 1 August 1914 only days before the outbreak of World War I. *The Endurance* was a sailing vessel with auxiliary steam power. The expedition included sailors and scientists.

Shackleton had intended to set up base camp on the Antarctic mainland at Vahsel Bay on the eastern shore of the Weddell Sea that stretches between longitude 20°W to 60°W and latitude 65°S to 75°S.

The Endurance entered pack ice on 7 December 1914 and sailed on south. Shackleton found the Weddell Sea filled with sea ice studded with icebergs. Sailing through it was slow and tedious work.

On 18 January 1915 when only thirty miles short of its objective, *The Endurance* became trapped in the sea ice. The ice in the Weddell Sea is churned in a perpetual clockwise motion by the westerly current that flows to the north of Antarctica and the ship was carried away from land in a north-westerly direction for the next nine months until 27 October 1915 when it was crushed by the ice, sinking three weeks later. All the men survived but were pitched onto the ice with only the stores and belongings they could save before the ship sank. Three of the ship's lifeboats were among the salvaged items.

For the next five months the men lived in tents, totally unprotected from the elements, on sea ice that is typically no more than two metres thick. During this period of great uncertainty Shackleton worked to maintain morale and optimism. He was ever watchful of the physical and mental state of all his people and drew close to him those he perceived as more in need of support. He also allocated people to each tent with great care so the personalities would gel and potential troublemakers would be neutralised. Shackleton and Wild rose early each day to prepare hot drinks for the whole crew.

On 9 April 1916 it was decided to launch the lifeboats and embark the expedition members to try to reach the nearest land. The three boats struggled through high seas and blizzards to a landing on Elephant Island a week later. This was their first landfall in 497 days.

Elephant Island was inhospitable and far from shipping lanes and sealers' routes. The only place on the island remotely suited to setting up camp was a spit of land that was totally exposed to the elements. Clearly Elephant Island was not a place they could stay and await rescue. So Shackleton decided to set out in the largest lifeboat with five of his companions and try to reach the whaling settlement on South Georgia Island.

Winter came early to the southern regions that year. Shackleton and his five companions embarked on 24 April and spent nearly four weeks sailing the open boat through the dark, storm-tossed Southern Ocean arriving at King Haakon Bay on South Georgia on 20 May, totally spent. During this voyage they weathered one of the worst winter storms to strike the area in years, one that caused much larger vessels to founder.

The privations of Shackleton and his men were not over. They had landed on the uninhabited side of the island and the whaling station of Stromness, where they could find help, was on the opposite side. Most of the crew was physically and mentally exhausted, debilitated and incapable of further effort. Shackleton could not contemplate trying to sail around to the whaling station with a debilitated crew in a barely seaworthy boat and with the ever-present risk of another storm. So he decided that he and two companions — Frank Worsley and Tom Crean — would walk across the mountainous uncharted interior of the island to seek rescue. This they did in a forced march of thirty-six hours without sleep and with minimal food. Their condition on arrival at the whaling station manager's house can be imagined, however it was such that one of the whalers who greeted them — a tough Norwegian hardened by years at sea — turned away and wept. A blizzard that would have finished them had it hit while they were on the march came down three hours after they arrived.

After much delay a rescue vessel was organised, first picking up the three men on the other side of South Georgia then going back to Elephant Island to rescue the remainder of the crew.

Despite the unspeakable hardships they endured during this odyssey, not one man was lost.

In accounts of this saga it is clear from the beginning that Shackleton cared deeply and with great intensity for his crew and was prepared to do anything to protect their physical and mental health. As the going got tougher Shackleton worked to maintain everyone's optimism and was always on the lookout for crewmen who were suffering more than others or whose spirits were flagging so he could keep these people close to him and give them extra attention and encouragement.

His story remains a shining beacon of care and one I believe every leader should know.

Bibliography

Gunningham N, Sinclair D, 2012, *Building Trust: OHS Management in the Mining Industry*, The National Research Centre for OHS Regulation, ANU, Canberra Australia.

Seppälä E, 2013, *Feeling It*, Psychology Today website, *http://www.psychologytoday.com/blog/feeling-it/201304/the-unexpected-benefits-compassion-business*, viewed 9 July 2019.

Leaders in Australia, 1996, the Australian Cultural Imprint for Leadership, Brighton, Victoria.

Simply the best Workplaces in Australia, 2003, Australian Centre for Industrial Relations research and Training (ACIRRT), University of Sydney, Sydney, Australia.

Atkins P, Parker S, 2012, *Understanding Individual Compassion in Organisations: the Role of Appraisals and Psychological Flexibility*, University of Western Australia, Perth, Western Australia.

Whittingham R, 2004, *The Blame Machine: Why Human Error Causes Accidents*, Elsevier Butterworth-Heinemann, Oxford, UK.

www.ingramcontent.com/pod-product-compliance
Lightning Source LLC
Chambersburg PA
CBHW022113210326
41597CB00047B/275